THE
GOLDEN OLDIE'S
GUIDEBOOK

Published by Peridot Press:
THE GAP YEAR GUIDEBOOK
THE BRILLIANT SCIENTIST'S GUIDEBOOK
THE GOLDEN OLDIE'S GUIDEBOOK

Due out in 1996 and 1997:
THE BRILLIANT MEDIA PERSON'S GUIDEBOOK
THE CAPTAIN OF INDUSTRY'S GUIDEBOOK

Copyright Peridot Press Ltd
First edition
Published in Great Britain 1995

ISBN 0 9519755 5 2

Peridot Press Ltd
2 Blenheim Crescent
London W11 1NN
Tel: 0171-221 7404

Printed in Great Britain by St Edmundsbury Press

THE
GOLDEN OLDIE'S
GUIDEBOOK

Editor and publisher • Rosamund McDougall

Researchers • James Forrester
Helen Walasek

Cover Design • Rose Pomeroy

Cartoons • Emma Broughton

Peridot Press

Acknowledgements

With many thanks to all the welfare organisations, voluntary workers and others who helped us with this new publication; to all the people who told us about their experiences; and to the health and social service experts who read through the final text to check its accuracy. For Peridot Press, special credit must go to researcher James Forrester, who has done most of the legwork in writing the book. Feedback from readers is always welcome: that way our books can be constantly improved.   *RMcD*

ARCHIE AND ANNIE
A few characters appear in this book when the mood takes us. Of course they bear no resemblance to any living persons. On the other hand...

Great-Uncle Archie Musket •	Retired Colonel, 85
Great-Aunt Annie Musket •	Sometime actress, 85
Fred Musket •	Son, architect in Canada, 53
The Niece •	Busy person with family, 45
The Niece's Husband •	Extremely busy person, 50

Preface

The idea for this book was conceived more than three years ago. Even in this short time, however, changes in the economy and the introduction of new legislation have radically affected people's prospects for old age. There is much that people over 50 need to keep informed about if they are to navigate their way through another 30 to 50 years.

So this year we got have got down to work to produce the first edition of THE GOLDEN OLDIE'S GUIDEBOOK. In it you will find more explanations about facts and figures than about feelings. You might also find a few jokes—and we apologise if we have not always been politically correct.

If this book concentrates on the work done by organisations rather than individuals, it is not because the devotion of countless friends and neighbours and families goes unrecognised by older people. It is simply something that cannot be put into words.   *Rosamund McDougall*

Contents

THEN

"All the world's a stage
And all the men and women merely players:
They have their exits and their entrances;
And one man in his time plays many parts,
His acts being seven ages...
...Last scene of all,
That ends this strange eventful history,
Is second childishness, and mere oblivion,
Sans teeth, Sans eyes, sans everything."

As You Like It, William Shakespeare

400 YEARS ON

"...Last scene of all,
That ends this strange eventful history,
Is contented dementia, and near-oblivion,
Teeth capped and bridged, eyes corneally grafted,
lens-lifted, inheritance planned,
All with logic Aristotelian."

Circular 5F 33/4BX, Geriatrica Department, DfH, Whitehall

A golden old age?

The ordering of this book has been carefully thought out. A quick read through the introductory paragraph to each chapter now may save time.

Who's old?

Look up the word 'old' in the thesaurus on a computer and it comes up with choices like battered, tattered, outmoded, passé and quaint. For those who felt passé at 20 and battered at 40, it is comforting to know that you can sometimes feel better at 60 and still be doing work you enjoy at 80. Older people are not an homogenous group. Their lives, interests and needs are as varied as those of any other age group. Most live thoroughly healthy and independent lives, but others need to be helped.

What do oldies need to know?

Political and economic trends do not seem quite as predictable as they used to be. In the 1990s people have seen their working lives become more erratic and the extent of state support for them when they retire is also in a constant state of flux. So although it is getting more difficult to plan ahead, it is becoming more important to try to do so.

INTRODUCTION

For the purposes of this book middle and old age is split into roughly three stages. Thinking ahead about physical and financial health is covered at age 50 in *Chapter 4: 50 Plus* which looks at fitness and sport, and in *Chapter 7: Money*. Apologies to those readers who know their way around these subjects already and don't need to find out more.

Needing to know about trends in government policy that affect old people, however, is vital: *Chapter 2: Curtain up* gives a glossary of some of the jargon involved. And even 40-somethings may find it useful to know—because they have ageing parents, perhaps—about developments in community care, retirement benefits, the NHS and private sector health care, which are covered in *Chapter 8: Community care and the social services; Chapter 9: Surviving in your own home; Chapter 10: Sheltered, residential care and nursing homes;* and *Chapter 11: Medical care* with *Chapter 12: Ailments and worse.*

For this group *Chapter 5: Organisations that help* gives information, addresses and telephone numbers for many of the charities and other organisations which offer practical help, advice and information.

Statisticians usually define old age as the period that begins with retirement, which for men means 65 and for women 60 (rising to 65 by the year 2020). Being described as 'elderly' can begin at 75 or 80, as it is usually this age group that is faced with difficult choices about whether to stay at home with extra support or move into sheltered housing or a residential care or nursing home: Chapters 8, 9, and 10 could be useful again.

Chapter 6: 65-100 Staying busy adds a few ideas for this older age group, listing some organisations that may not already be known. *Chapter 11: Medical care* and *Chapter 12: Ailments and worse* summarise the most common ailments and illnesses suffered in old age, giving details of organisations that help and pinpointing research developments where possible.

Finally, for anyone brave enough to want to know, there is *Chapter 13: Funerals, burials and cremation.*

The vocabulary of dealing with old age is so complicated that it is worth revising from time to time. Trying to learn it for the first time at 90 could bring your final curtain down with a bump.

Long-term terminology

Here is a glossary of some of the terms you will find used in this book. They refer to institutions, policies, methodology and job descriptions. Where the jargon is particularly new or complicated, a more detailed explanation is given in the chapter referred to.

A

ABBEYFIELD Type of sheltered housing. See Chapter 10.

ADL (Activities for daily living) TESTS. See Chapter 7.

ASSESSMENT If you are an oldie with problems, you will have a lot of these. Whether you are asking for social services or an equipment

CURTAIN UP: THE JARGON

grant, or considering going into a nursing home, you will be assessed by someone who asks you a lot of questions before they decide what you need. See Chapters 8, 9, 10, 11 and 12.

B

BENEFITS A benefit is usually a weekly payment you can collect from the post office. For example, income support. For benefits which old or disabled people can claim, see Chapter 7.

BENEFITS AGENCY The executive arm of the Department of Social Security. It deals with paying benefits.

C

CARE ASSESSMENT What happens when a social service department assesses Granny's situation at home to see if, for example, she can cut her own toenails. See Chapter 8.

CARE ASSISTANT Or Care Attendant. New name for what used to be called a Home Help. Both are CARE WORKERS.

CARE CENTRE, DAY Where Great-Uncle Archie can get parked and entertained for the day when Great-Aunt Annie can't cope and needs a break. Needs to be arranged through social services.

CARED-FOR The cared-for is the old and frail person (among others) who should be looked after by all the CARERS and CARE WORKERS.

CARE FEE PLAN A financial plan to cover the costs of staying in a residential or nursing home.

CARE PLAN This is the plan or timetable a social services department draws up to help you (as an old person) survive.

CARER A carer is someone, usually a relative, who looks after an old, ill or disabled person who cannot look after himself . The demands made of a carer are usually continuous and very great, and involve regular responsibilities like feeding and bathing the other person.

CARER SUPPORT WORKER Someone who supports the CARER. Could be a social worker who arranges for the carer to have a break. See Chapter 8.

CARE WORKER A paid outsider who comes in to help with house-work or carry out other tasks that do not need nursing qualifications.

CURTAIN UP: THE JARGON

CHARITY, REGISTERED See Chapter 5.

*CLIENT This word is now used to cover anyone who is using a social
or health service. Can cover a wide range of politically correct or
incorrect words ranging from patient to lunatic.*

*COMMUNITY CARE LEGISLATION Policies aimed at looking
after people in their own homes rather than in hospitals, residential
or nursung homes. See Chapters 8-11.*

COMMUNITY HEALTH COUNCIL (CHC) See Chapter 11.

*COMMUNITY NURSE A nurse who works from a clinic or other
non-hospital setting.*

*COMPLAINTS PROCEDURES Details of these are given in most
chapters.*

*CONTRIBUTIONS AGENCY The executive arm of the Department
of Social Security that deals with National Insurance. See Chapter 3.*

D

*DISTRICT HEALTH AUTHORITY Responsible for assessing
community health needs and providing the relevant care services. See
Chapter 11.*

DISTRICT NURSE See Chapter 11.

*DISABLED No agreement on definition (but you can have your
disability measured by techniques that classify you as, say, 80 per
cent disabled). References in most chapters.*

*DOMICILIARY CARE Personal care (like bathing) carried out for
older people in their own homes, usually by care workers sent by
social service departments. Could be a growth market.*

E

*ELDERLY Definitions vary. Unless otherwise stated, it refers in this
book to people over 75 or over 65 if they have serious disabilities.*

F

*FUNERAL PRE-PAYMENT PLAN Pre-paid plans which allow
people to cover their future funeral costs (based on todays'
prices) and so spare their relatives the financial burden of
organising a funeral. See Chapter 13.*

13

CURTAIN UP: THE JARGON

G

GENERAL PRACTITIONER (GP)   *The family doctor—as opposed to GP Fundholders (see below) ordinary GPs are answerable to their District Health Authority.*

GOLDEN OLDIE   Oldie with attitude.

GP FUNDHOLDER   *A GP whose practice has an annual budget that is used to pay for staff, prescriptions, and community and hospital services. GP fundholders get their money from, and are answerable to, the local Family Health Services Authority.*

GRANT   *As used in this book, a sum of money given by a government body, local authority or charitable foundation on a one-off basis for a particular purpose. For example, Housing Grant (See Chapter 9), or Disabled Facilities Grant (See Chapter 7).*

H

HEALTH AUTHORITY   *See District Health Authority (above).*
HEALTH VISITOR   *See Chapter 11.*
HOSPICE   *Special hospital for those with (usually) terminal illness. See Chapter 11.*

I

INCONTINENCE   *The inability to control either the bladder or the bowel or both. An undignified condition. See Chapter 12.*
INTERNAL MARKET   *New way of organising former public institutions, ranging from the BBC to the National Health Service. What happens is that divisions, departments and units price their own goods and services for sale and bid for the best value goods and services they need, either within the organisation or outside it. See Chapter 3.*

L

LOCAL AUTHORITY   *Refers to a local metropolitan borough council, county council or unitary local government authority (not to be confused with HEALTH AUTHORITY). See Chapter 8.*

CURTAIN UP: THE JARGON

M

MINICOM   *Special telephone service for people who are hard of hearing.*

N

NURSING HOME   *Homes which provide 24-hour nursing care.*

NHS HOSPITAL TRUSTS   *These are hospitals which have corporate status, with their own management controlling the trust's assets and budgets.*

O

OCCUPATIONAL THERAPIST   *Occupational therapists help people to cope with the varying physical demands of daily living. See Chapter 9.*

OLD AGE PENSIONER (OAP)   *Someone who has reached state retirement age—60 for women, 65 for men.*

OLDER   *No-one can agree where old age begins and no-one likes being described as old. People who used to be described as old are now sometimes referred to as older or elderly. Statisticallly, 'older' can begin at 65 and 'elderly' at 75.*

OLDIE   *Older people brave enough to admit they are not always quite what they used to be.*

P

PENSION, STATE RETIREMENT (SRP)   *What you get (not much) if you paid your National Insurance stamps for long enough. See Chapter 7.*

PENSIONS, PRIVATE   *See Chapter 7.*

PRESSURE GROUP   *Organisations that lobby the government, in this case for reforms of legislation affecting older people. For example, Age Concern, Carers National Association, Help the Aged. See Chapters 3 and 5.*

POWER OF ATTORNEY   *See Chapter 7.*

PRIMARY HEALTH CARE   *Care provided in the community by GP's, opticians and dentists.*

CURTAIN UP: THE JARGON

R

*RESPITE   A break. In the context of oldies, a rest from looking after
Granny when her dementia is driving you demented.*

*RESIDENTIAL CARE HOME   provides 24 hours-a-day personal
care.*

*RETIREMENT HOUSING   Bungalows, cottages or flats designed for
the active retired or elderly person.*

S

*SECONDARY HEALTH CARE   This takes place in clinics and
community health centres.*

SHELTERED HOUSING   See Chapter 10.

*SOCIAL SERVICE DEPARTMENT, SOCIAL SERVICES, SOCIAL
WORKER   See Chapter 8.*

T

*THIRD AGE   A term used to describe the third part of possibly four
stages in life, but without a clear dividing line. Say 60 to 75.*

*TOP-UP FUNDING   Extra money used to bridge the gap between
what the state pays for and the full cost of private residential and
nursing home fees. Sometimes provided by charities.*

V

*VOLUNTARY ORGANISATIONS   Organisations begun by people
in response to a need not met by any official organisation. Usually
registered charities. See Chapter 5.*

W

*WILL   The document that determines who gets your money, house
and other possessions after you die. See Chapter 7.*

WOOPIE   Wealthy Older Person. Not many left round here.

DEPARTMENTS
EDUCATION
ENVIRONMENT
HEALTH
SOCIAL SECURITY
SOCIAL SE
HOU
A
PRE
CHAR
ORGA

3

The framework

Government ministries, local authorities, the health service, charities, private agencies and businesses supply a mass of information about what they do for older people. Much of it is distilled in other sections of this book. But for the next generation of older people it is just as important to understand the constantly shifting political and economic background. This section explains the framework of institutions that make relevant policy and carry it out.

The numbers game

There are many reasons why older people are so often described as a problem. Perhaps the main one is that people are living longer.

In 1961 there were 11.7 million people aged 65 and over in the UK, representing nearly 12 per cent of the population. By 1991 the numbers had grown to 15.7 million and made up 16 per cent of the total population. According to the 1994 volume of *Social Trends*, the government's annual statistical snapshot of life in Britain, by the year 2031 the proportion of over 65s is expected to be 22 per cent of the total UK population.

Clearly, most of these older people will be willing and able to

17

THE FRAMEWORK

BRITAIN'S GREYING POPULATION
Thousands (% of total)

	1971	1981	1991	1993	Proj 2001	Proj 2011
Age 45-59	9,959	9,313	9,259	9,818	-	-
Age 60-64	3,148	2,867	2,818	2,769	-	-
Age 65-74	4,658	5,079	4,948	5,046	-	-
Age 75-84	2,109	2,620	3,070	2,953	-	-
85 and over	476	589	878	964	-	-
Total	54,388	54,815	56,207	56,559	58,133	59,548

Source: Office of Population Censuses and Surveys

organise their own lives. One in three people aged 65 and over are even able to help other people, according to a study that formed part of the government's *General household survey* in 1991. But a minority will have special needs that have to be met. They will tend to be concentrated, though not exclusively, in the over-80s age group which has grown from 1.9 million in 1961 to 3.7 million in 1991 and which is projected to be 6.9 million by the year 2031.

Financial uncertainty

Older and soon-to-be old people already face circumstances which many find alarmingly uncertain. Far from the expectation of a secure retirement with a house, an adequate pension and guaranteed free health care from the state for the rest of life, there are now fears that the state will not provide, that savings will be eaten up by residential or nursing home or medical fees, and that fellow citizens will be less willing to support them.

One reason for recent worries is the move from providing free hospital long-stay beds for those too frail to cope alone at home. Instead, there is a national policy to return people to community care, and to make them pay for necessary residential or nursing home beds if they cannot manage in their own homes. The effects of recent changes in the health service and in the development of community care are dealt with in detail in Chapters 8-11.

No-one to help?

This switch is taking place against a background of changing family circumstances. Few modern homes offer enough space for grandparents to stay or live. There are fewer younger people to care for an increasing number of older ones. Wives and daughters who used to look after dependent parents are now more likely to go out to work and may be less willing to endanger their marriages by taking on what might become a stressful burden. Those who look after sick relatives are often exhausted and short of money—because they cannot earn a living at the same time. In every village, town and city there are still kind neighbours who help. But although most older people are still cared for by their relatives, the traditional, localised and extended family is now smaller and scattered, and often less able to help.

Gently downhill

For most people, old age means a gradual physical deterioration over many years. A supplement to the 1991 *General Household*

LIVING ALONE

An increasing number of really old people, most of them women whose husbands have died, live alone. In 1991, 58 per cent of people aged 85 and over lived alone. Of all people aged 65 and over who live alone, a very small proportion receive any help from health and social services. In 1991, one in ten had a home help, mostly for only one or two hours a week; 3 per cent had meals on wheels, and 6 per cent had a district nurse or health visitor.
General Household Survey, 1991

THE FRAMEWORK

Survey showed that the vast majority continue to live in the community : 38 per cent live alone; 39 per cent with an elderly spouse and 6 per cent with a son or daughter. Between 1981 and 1991 the proportion of over 65s living permanently in hospitals or in residential and nursing homes rose from 5 per cent to 7 per cent.

This is believed to reflect not so much a greater need by older people as the simple fact that the number of private residential care and nursing homes mushroomed in the 1980s in response to changes in social security rules. The expansion of private homes was encouraged when these rules were altered to allow the state to meet most of the cost of private residential care or nursing home fees. The social security budget spent £10 million on these fees in 1979, but by 1993, when the new community care rules came in, the total had risen to more than £2 billion.

Defining national policy

Only a minority of older people have special needs. How they are met is a matter of public policy in which finance and geography play major roles. Centrally, the government defines national policy, sometimes guided by international conventions as well as by presumptions about the needs of the home population.

The government places the main responsibility for providing for older people's health needs on the National Health Service and for their needs in the community on local authorities (*see Chapter 8*). In recent years, official policy has led increasingly to the functions of both the NHS and local government being split into 'provider' and 'purchaser' roles. This kind of jargon tends to obscure what is happening on the ground and makes it more difficult to understand where you should go for help.

Internal markets

What it means in the NHS, for example, is that local health authorities no longer provide directly the hospitals, clinics and other medical services people need. Instead, they assess the health needs of the local population and plan to provide the appropriate services by 'buying' them from 'providers' like hospital trusts.

Similarly, local councils used to provide a wide range of services, like residential homes, day centres and meals on wheels. Now, increasingly they pay private agencies and voluntary organisations to provide the care services local people need.

Whose responsibility?

Only a minority of older people receive help with their daily needs from local social services, and there is growing evidence that the health service is rationing medical care for older people. Of course, families have always been the main carers for older people. They are clearly expected to continue doing so although official policy does accept some responsibility for providing services that older people may need. At this point it might be useful to describe who is responsible for what.

Government

The lives of older people cross most government departments or ministries, but the key ones involved in defining policy in relation to their special needs are :

DEPARTMENT OF HEALTH
Department of Health (DoH)　　　　　　**Tel: 0171-210 5983**
Richmond House, 79 Whitehall, London SW1A 2NS

This ministry is responsible for both the NHS and for community care policy. It is also responsible for defining the regulations governing the provision of many services for older people, including residential care and nursing homes. The DoH also has a broad inspection role, which includes investigating the facilities provided by local health and social services authorities and defining the inspection function of local councils.

DEPARTMENT OF SOCIAL SECURITY
Department of Social Security (DSS)　　　**Tel: 0171-210 5983**
Richmond House, 79 Whitehall, London SW1A 2NS

Responsible for national policy on pensions and benefits. Day-to-day management and administration is devolved to the

21

THE FRAMEWORK

Contributions Agency for *national insurance* (pensions and other non–means tested benefits) and to the Benefits Agency for social security, including *income support*.

DEPARTMENT OF THE ENVIRONMENT
Department of the Environment (DoE)　　　　**Tel: 0171-276 0900**
2 Marsham Street, London SW1P 3EBT

Responsible for national housing policy, including home improvement grants and disabled facilities grants.

DEPARTMENT FOR EDUCATION
Department for Education (DfE)　　　　**Tel: 0171-925 5000**
Sanctuary Buildings, Great Smith Street
Westminster, London SW1P 3BTT

Responsible for national policy on education, including adult education which is devolved to local education authorities.

Local government
Local authority services are described in detail in Chapter 8. The key departments dealing with the needs of older people are :

Social services departments
These are *social work departments* in Scotland and *health and social services boards* in Northern Ireland. Local authorities are still bound by the 1948 *National Assistance Act*, which requires them to provide a range of services for older people. On top of this, the *NHS and Community Care Act* 1990 requires them to assess the need for services of each of their clients. Once this assessment has been made the local authority is now legally obliged to provide these services (although some local authorities are contesting the legality of their obligations to provide services which they say they have no money to pay for). Services include help in the home like meals-on-wheels and domiciliary care (home helps); provision of facilities like day centres and luncheon clubs; and assessments of need for community care. It is these assessments that now lead to decisions about whether people should have a

high degree of help in the home or whether they should go into residential care or nursing homes. Increasingly, local councils contract out the provision of many of these services to private agencies and voluntary organisations.

Housing departments

These are responsible for providing the range of 'social' housing needed by local people who either cannot afford to buy or can no longer manage without help. This responsibility includes sheltered housingfor older people and those with disabilities who are still broadly independent but need some care.

Education departments

Although further and higher education are now the responsibility of independent funding councils, local authorities retain some responsibility for providing adult education.

Other organisations

Among five other types of organisation there are three types of voluntary organisation concerned with the special needs of older people, although they tend to overlap. Your local council, library and advice agencies should have lists of those in your area.

Charities

Many of the charities that provide services specifically for older people work increasingly on contract to local social services authorities, and sometimes to a local health authority. Examples of these are Crossroads Care, which provides care attendants (home helps) to look after older people in their own homes so that the person who normally takes responsibility can get a break; and Age Concern, which provides bathing services for old people in their own homes. *See Chapter 5.*

Pressure groups

These lobby politicians and campaign through the media for new or amended laws on issues like disability, pensions, allowances, grants or benefits. Some are also involved in local campaigning and give advice directly to older people; for example, Age Concern, the Carers National Association, and Help the Aged.

THE FRAMEWORK

Self-help organisations

These are cooperative organisations formed by older people themselves to campaign for a better deal. They include pensioner organisations and trade union retired members associations. There is a National Pensioners Conventions Council covering many of these organisations.

Other bodies: think tanks

These do not directly or specifically help older people, but are useful to know about if you plan to be an actively lobbying oldie, because they sometimes carry out research that can be used as evidence to back a case. Examples include The Policy Studies Institute (general) and the specialist Centre for Policy on Ageing.

Other bodies: commercial agencies

Private sector agencies have mushroomed in recent years, partly in response to government policies that stipulated that 85 per cent of the *special transitional grant* made from social security funds to local authorities to help them set up community care have had to be spent spent in the independent sector. Private companies now own and run many residential care and nursing homes and are beginning to develop domiciliary services like home helps and meals on wheels. *See Chapter 8.*

A caring community?

There has been widespread agreement for several decades that older people in need of care should be looked after as far as possible in their own homes. As long ago as 1963, the Ministry of Health defined the aims of community care in the following terms :

"Elderly people living at home may need special support to enable them to cope with their infirmities and to prevent their isolation from society. As their capabilities diminish, they will more often require such services as home help, laundry services, meals cooked ready for eating and chiropody. Loss of mobility brings the need for friendly visiting, transport to social clubs and occupation centres, and arrangements for holidays. When illness is added to other infirmities, they need more home nursing, night care, and help generally in the home. In terminal illness, an elderly person may for a limited period need considerable help from many of the domiciliary services."

But, in both the NHS and in community care, what services are available often depends crucially on where you live and on whether or not there is an active local pressure group.

This is because, while the ideal spelt out in 1963 has been accepted by successive governments ever since, the extra resources needed to produce that level of care in the community has never been voted through. Each of the services listed in the 1963 Ministry of Health statement is clearly defined in law as the responsibility of local councils. But there are enough let-out clauses to make it a matter for local discretion.

By mid-1995 the health service and local authorities were beginning to clarify who was financially responsible for looking after elderly people. Meanwhile, cases of ageing parents having to sell the family home to pay for residential or nursing home fees—where previously they would have been able to stay in an NHS bed—have given rise to bitter debate. *See Chapters 9, 10 and 11.*

People with disability

The only group which can claim that a local council must help them is people with disabilities who have been assessed as having a need for a service spelt out in Section 2 of the *Chronically Sick and Disabled Persons Act* 1970. That claim has been tested in the courts which have ruled that local councils cannot use lack of resources as a reason to deny a disabled person a necessary service if that need continues.

The snag is that even this right applies only to people the council itself assesses as 'severely disabled'. Of course, a high proportion of people with severe disabilities will be over retirement age. But as a group, most older people cannot be described as 'severely disabled'.

Even that guarantee is not available in the health service although it is supposed to provide medical care from 'the cradle

THE FRAMEWORK

to the grave'. In fact, the courts have ruled that what the health service must provide is constrained by available resources under the 1977 *National Health Service Act*. In other words, a local health authority can argue that it cannot provide a particular service because it has run out of money.

Patchy services

So, although public policy aims at stopping older people going into residential homes or hospitals if they can manage at home with the right support, in practice the community care services have not always materialised: many people, therefore have had no choice but to go into a home at their own or their family's expense. Nor have sufficient facilities been provided in the community for people leaving long–stay hospitals, which began to close in 1986.

In fact, services in the community have developed piecemeal, while there has been an enormous expansion in private residential care and nursing homes. This expansion came after social security rules were changed to allow most of the cost of private residential care or nursing home fees to be met.

This huge increase in the social security budget was one of the main reasons for the changes to community care policies. It was not just the rising cost that mattered. There was also widespread concern that the aim of keeping older people in their own homes for as long as possible was being thwarted. The system changed in April 1993, when responsibility for paying the fees was transferred from the Department of Social Security to local authorities.

This has been said to increase choice for older people. But the change means that the system has changed from one that is open–ended to one that is cost-limited. In other words, people who qualified for help under the old system were guaranteed that all or most of their home fees would be met by social security. Now, whether the fees will be met depends on whether the local council has enough money left to meet them.

THE FRAMEWORK

The new system

The new system has introduced several changes. For the first time, older people have their needs assessed before decisions are made about whether they can be looked after at home or need to go into a residential care or nursing home. If they have assets of more than £8,000, these must be used to meet the cost of fees in a home. If they have less than £8,000 they can choose which home they go into, provided they can find ways of paying to top up what their local council is prepared to pay (*see Chapter 10*).

Money has now been made available to councils specifically for domiciliary care. That should mean that older people are more likely to be offered help to keep them in their own homes. In practice, the cost of this is so high that many councils have introduced capping on community care packages. They are also introducing, or raising, charges for services like meals-on-wheels and home helps. If this process is extrapolated, there may soon be little difference between what you pay a local authority for home care services (having already paid council tax) and what you pay if you go directly to commercial agencies.

Typically councils pay the cost of services in the home only up to the level of the equivalent residential care or nursing home fees. This means that the older person must either cope with services that are admitted to be less than they need or find the necessary extra cash from their own pockets, or from family or charities.

Councils are now also required to take account of the views of their clients (council taxpayers) and their carers in drawing up community care plans. This should mean that services are more responsive to people's needs, rather than the ideas of professionals of what they should be.

Working with health services

The new community care system is also supposed to ensure that people are not discharged from hospital before the services they need at home are available. There have been several cases where older people have been discharged home where this has not happened and arguments have arisen about the health service's responsibility for continuing care.

At least one court case has resulted and a new circular has been issued by the Department of Health *(see Chapter 11)*. This asks local health authorities to consider the likely need for in-patient continuing care and to draw up and publish local policies which will also define who is eligible for what service. This emphasis on local policies has raised objections that the 'National' is being removed from the National Health Service. However, the publication of local health policies will give people a yardstick against which to judge whether they are getting the services they need.

Making a complaint

If you think your local health and social services are not providing proper care for older people there are several avenues of complaint.

Social services departments in England and Wales are required to produce annual community care plans. By April 1986, English authorities are also required to introduce local community care charters. These can be used to attempt to obtain the services in the home that older people need.

Local councils publish formal complaints procedures, but it can sometimes help to get your local councillor to have the case reviewed first. You can find the names of local councillors from the town hall. Your local MP may also be able to help if you are not satisfied with the results. If you suspect there has been maladministration, you can also ask the local government ombudsman to review the case.

If your complaint is about the health service, you can complain to the local hospital direct using the Patient's Charter or any local charters as your yardstick. You can also ask your local Community Health Council to take up the case. CHCs are watchdog bodies whose function is to monitor the health service on behalf of the public. Your local MP or councillors may again be able to help. If you are not satisfied, your complaint may be referred to the health service ombudsman. *See Chapters 9 and 11.*

4

50 plus: Staying fit

Few people of 50 think they are old. They are not. But half-way through a century can be a good time to take stock and think about the years ahead. Health checks are a good idea—physical and financial—and it is not too late to reform bad habits. Some say that the 'Third Age', beginning at 50, is the best.

Keeping fit

With the passage of time, everyone's physical capabilities gradually alter. This alteration is due to three things: chronic disease, such as heart disease, bronchitis and arthritis; natural decline of muscular strength; and decline due to disuse. Often a deterioration in health is wrongly attributed to age when it is in fact due to under-use of the body's muscles.

There is nothing to stop over-50s taking exercise, providing it is started carefully and slowly. Half-an-hour of aerobics could be lethal for someone who has not exercised for a year. At the other

29

50 PLUS: STAYING FIT

extreme, 272 people over 60 took part in the 26-mile 1995 London Marathon and survived.

Muscling up

With increasing age it is important to maintain muscle strength in order to cope with the demands of daily life. Age is associated with the gradual loss of muscle strength, joint mobility and stamina. Although some loss of muscle is inevitable, most of this age-related loss is due to underuse of the muscles, and suitable and moderate exercise can reverse such deterioration.

...even with illness

The benefits of exercise can be enjoyed not only by those who have lead too sedentary a life, but also by those with the chronic problems of middle or old age, such as bronchitis and arthritis. Arthritic joints cannot be cured by exercise, but gentle movement will help to keep the joints lubricated and prevent them from weakening. The exercises of particular benefit to those with arthiritis are swimming and flexibility classes.

Chronic bronchitis is common in older age groups, especially among smokers, and those with a chronic (bronchitic) cough may not realise how much their exercise capacity is already limited by the narrowed airways in their lungs. This damage is irreversible and exercise will not cure it. However with medically advised training such respiratory difficulties can be eased.

Exercise provides specific health benefits as well, such as reducing the chances of developing diabetes or, by helping the

Medical checklist

There are some physical conditions that you should consult your doctor about before you exercise:

- If you have been told previously by a doctor that you have heart trouble.
- If you are over 65 and are unaccustomed to vigorous exercise.
- If you suffer from swollen feet and /or take diuretics.
- If you develop a pain in the chest on exertion.
- If you experience feelings of faintness, spells of dizziness and/or palpitations.
- If you have arthritis or a bone or joint problem which has been or could be aggravated by exercise.
- If you have active gout.
- If you have severe disorders of the veins in the leg, such as gross varicose veins.
- If you have Diabetes Mellitus, whether it requires insulin treatment or not.
- If you have chronic bronchitis, emphysema or a regular morning cough.
- Gross obesity.

"Fifty Plus, All to play for", by Prof. P.H. Fentem, & Dr E.J. Bassey of Nottingham University. Published by the Sports Council (1994).

heart to work more efficiently,the risk of increased blood pressure.

A research programme run by Professor P.H. Fentem and Doctor E.J. Bassey when they were at Manchester University also found that a group of regularly exercising older people were not only fitter, but also showed much less mental decline than averagely unfit people of the same age. (*Benefits of Exercise: the evidence* Manchester University Press 1990).

Health check

However, before embarking on a programme of regular exercise you should have your initial level of fitness assessed; this may require talking to your doctor to make sure you have no medical problems. A higher level of fitness can be achieved only with time, and improved health cannot be reached by trying to speed up what is a gradual process. It is very important not to over-exercise. 'Going for the burn' will do much more serious damage than just causing the aches and pains that prevent further exercise. Similarly staying healthy requires regular exercise, not a frenzied bout of activity every now and then.

Cold sweat

When exercising you should expect to notice that you are breathing more deeply than usual, feeling warm, sweating a little, and that your muscles are working more than usual. However you should stop exercising if you get any pain in your chest, neck and upper left arm or legs, or if you break into a cold sweat, feel faint or dizzy, or suffer from distressing or prolonged breathlessness, or extreme or prolonged tiredness.

Making too many demands

Suddenly making too many demands of your body can lead to an accident and injury; whether that be cardiovascular, such as a heart attack, or orthopaedic, such as damage to muscle or bone. According to John Brewer of the Lillishaw Human Performance Centre, however, "the inevitable negative potential for injury

---

Fitness assessment

To assess initial fitness, Professor Fentem and Doctor Bassey suggest a series of questions like these:

- Do you struggle for breath even after running a short distance?
- Does your heart pound after a few flights of stairs?
- Do you ache all over after digging a small patch of garden or mowing the lawn?
- Are you exhausted after an hour of housework?
- Are you tired out after carrying two bags of shopping for a quarter of a mile?
- Is it an effort to bend and tie your shoelaces?

If the answers are "Yes", you have probably led a very sedentary life and are unused to any form of exercise. If this is the case then it is important to begin exercising gently.

---

that people always cite as an excuse (for not exercising) is far out-weighed by the positive aspects for the heart and lungs. Also, psychologically a healthy body creates a healthy mind."

An affair of the heart

Mr. Brewer goes on to say that a lot of people concentrate on what muscle groups they use in exercise, and tend to overlook the fact that the most important muscle that needs to be exercised is your heart. The golden rule is to build up the level of exercise and its duration in very small steps, perhaps adjusting your exercise pro-gramme every four or five weeks.

It is important that you choose an exercise that you enjoy and that is readily to hand. Trying to swim regularly can be a problem if the nearest swimming pool is ten miles away. It is also impor-tant to gear your exercises not only to what is available, but to your own capabilities. According to John Brewer you should not set your initial exercise level too high and only exercise to a "tol-erable level of discomfort."

Mix and match

Although improvements in fitness may be imperceptible during each session they will become apparent over several weeks. Keeping fit, strong and supple, however, requires a mix of differ-ing exercises that promote strength, stamina and flexibility. These need to happen more than once a week to be effective.

It is important to gear your exercises not only to your wishes, but to your needs and capabilities. Swimming provides good all-round exercise because it supports the body while using a large variety of muscles. Walking and jogging develop leg muscles and stamina but little else. Keep fit, music and movement exercises are also useful because they provide for a variety of activities and muscle use, and can help to maintain or improve flexibility, co-ordination and balance.

GOLDEN OLDIE

Eighty-eight-year-old Mavis Lindstrom was one of many older entrants in the 1994 London Marathon. She completed the 26-mile course in about nine and a half hours. Was Ms Lindstrom a professional runner? No, and she only started at 62.

Diet

It is not just regular exercise that leads to better health. A more considered diet can also help to alleviate the problems associated with growing older. The Exercise Association of Great Britain offers a few helpful dietary hints in its leaflet *Mobilistics: Fitness for the over 50s.*

- Avoid adding salt to your food, as this can help to keep your blood pressure down.
- Drink alcohol only in moderation (21 units a week, not a day, for men and 14 units a week for women). Here a 'unit' is taken to be equal to one standard measure of alcohol: half a pint of beer
  or a glass of wine, or one shot of spirits.
- Base your diet on carbohydrates such as wholemeal bread, pasta, rice, potatoes, beans and peas. In addition, oil rich fish or its equivalents, like cod liver oil, may help to reduce joint stiffness.

High-fat diets are linked to heart and circulation problems. Choose semi-skimmed milk rather than full-cream milk. Cut down on foods that are high in animal fats and choose lean cuts of meat and poultry. Use oils rich in monosaturated or polyunsaturated fats like olive oil or sunflower oil for cooking. Similarly, use a low-fat spread instead of ordinary margarine or butter.

Eating low-fat dairy products, along with green leafy vegetables, salads, citrus fruits and carbohydrates will replenish your vitamin C and E and increase the levels of calcium in your body to help prevent brittle bones. Also eating fresh fruit and vegetables can combat tiredness. Lack of iron is a prime cause of fatigue and can be prevented by eating vegetables and fruit, especially spinach, broccoli and dried apricots.

Good sport

Those who have regularly played tennis or golf, continue to ski or practise other sports need no new ideas. The following list is largely for oldies and townies who want to try something new (with apologies to anyone who would rather be dead than doing some of these activities). As well as the various national organisations which offer advice on leisure activities, there are usually good sources of information in libraries and leisure centres about what is going on locally.

Amateur Athletics Association of Great Britain   **Tel: 0121-440 5000**
225A Bristol Road, Edgbaston
Birmingham B5 7UB

The Sports Council   **Tel: 0171-388 1277**
16 Upper Woburn Place
London WC1H OQP

The Sports Council publishes the addresses of a whole range of sporting and activity organisations in its *Governing bodies of sport address book*. It can also provide information on local amenities and medical advice.

Archery

Like golf, archery can be enjoyed by anyone aged between nine and ninety. The sport, with its repeated drawing and release of the bow, provides a way of improving the heart's condition in a cycle of effort and relaxation. Throughout the course of an archery competition a person will also walk roughly three-and-a half miles to collect arrows from the target. Unlike golf, however, if you feel unable or unwilling to do this your arrows can always be collected and scored by other competitors; and you do have time between rounds to relax as you wait for other people to take their turn.

50 PLUS: STAYING FIT

The Grand National Archery Society has 22,000 members in 1,100 clubs throughout the UK, as well as 65 archery clubs for disabled members. The annual society membership fee is £18 but there is an additional club fee which can be anything from £30 to £60, depending on whether the club is based in the country or the city. To find out about where your nearest archery club is, just write to the GNAS.

The Grand National Archery Society　　　　　**Tel: 01203-696 631**
The National Agriculture Centre
Stoneleigh, Kenilworth, Warwickshire CV8 2LG

Bowls

Fans of bowling describe it as a game people can play from cradle to grave. There are two types of bowls, indoor and outdoor, and you can compete either individually, in pairs, or as fours in club bowls. The object is to get your bowls as close to the jack as possible. The English Bowling Association (the EBA, for out-door-playing men) estimates that about half its 30,000 members fall into the 40 to 60 age bracket, with the rest falling equally either side. There are at present roughly 2,700 bowls clubs throughout the 35 counties affiliated to the EBA.

The game lasts two to three hours so stamina is needed. But according to Arthur Meeson of the EBA, 'as little as five per cent of the game is actually spent bending over and delivering the bowl.' The rest of the time a player can watch the action, work out how to play the next shot, or just sit down.

The English Bowling Association　　　　　**Tel: 01903-820 022**
Lyndhurst Road, Worthing
West Sussex BN11 2AZ

Keep fit exercises

Keep fit, music and movement exercises are useful because they provide for a variety of activities and muscle use, and can help to not only increase fitness but maintain or improve flexibility, co-ordination and balance, so reducing the possibility of falls and

36

BEER, BOSOMS & BOWLS

Charlie May celebrated his 100th birthday by going down to the Northaw Cuffley Bowling Club to play. For his 90th birthday he had been given a new set of bowls, but that wasn't enough. So besotted was May with bowling that on his 96th birthday he asked a doctor to amputate an arthritic finger because it was interfering with his game. When asked by a church minister what the secret of his longevity was, twice-married May answered "beer, bosoms and bowls." He lived to 102 and the club holds a Charlie May memorial match every year.

---

broken bones. There is an almost endless variety of keep fit exercise programmes, such as aerobics, circuit training, and aqua-aerobics, that exercise the heart and lungs as well as various muscle groups. Usually well-supervised classes are available at local leisure centres or private health and fitness clubs. Or you can get a leaflet showing exercises to do in your own home:

The Exercise Association of Great Britain   **Tel: 0171-278 0811**
Unit 4, Angel Gate
326 City Road, London EC1V 2PT

Golf

Golf is an enormously popular sport, played by hundreds of thousands of people of all ages all over the UK. Depending on how many holes are to be played, a golfer can get or stay fit by regularly walking two miles or more. The swing of the golf club itself can help keep hips, back, neck and shoulders flexible; and driving, putting and chipping can maintain and develop coordination. The game can be played at your own pace.

The English Golf Union   **Tel: 0116-255 3042**
1-3 Upper King Street, Leicester LE1 6XF

50 PLUS: STAYING FIT

Orienteering

Orienteering is a 'country walk with a difference', a sport where competitors navigate their way at their own pace between features marked on a special coloured map. The main orienteering season runs from September to May or June, with a lessening of activity in December and January. It is a good way to get or stay fit while exploring the countryside and seeing places you would not usually visit.

Orienteering is well established throughout the UK, and anyone wishing to take up the sport is sure to find a club nearby which will give advice and encouragement to any newcomer, no matter what their age. British Orienteering Federation statistics published at the end of 1994 showed that of the federation's 7,182 members, 1,767 were aged 50 and over. To find your local orienteering club all you need to do is to send a 12" by 9" SAE marked *general information pack* to the British Orienteering Federation.

British Orienteering Federation (BOF)   **Tel: 01629- 734 042**
Riverside, Dale Road North
Matlock, Derbyshire DE4 2HX

Swimming

Indoor swimming is the next most popular form of exercise after walking. Like walking it encourages stamina but it also uses a wider variety of joints and muscles. The muscles are exercised while working against the resistance of the water, which also supports the body and so lessens the stress on the joints that may occur while walking or jogging. The constant pressure exerted equally around the body by the water improves blood circulation. If you want to swim more competitively, many swimming clubs throughout the UK have a Masters section, in which competitors are usually grouped in five-year age bands up to the final age group, in England, of 80+ years.

The Amateur Swimming Association   **Tel: 01509- 230 431**
Harold Fern House, Derby Square
Loughborough, Leics LE11 0AL

TARZAN
Unluckily Chester Kozlowski, 87, was drawn against Johnny Weissmuller in the 100 metres freestyle heats at the 1928 Olympic games. Weissmuller won the medals, then auditioned for Tarzan, and went on to win Jane by swinging from tropical trees. Does Kozlowski have any regrets? It seems not. He still swims every day, and was due to compete in the 100 metres backstroke, 50 metres and 100 metres breaststroke and the 50 metres freestyle at the 1995 British National Championships at Crystal Palace.
Kozlowski still holds the world record in his age group for the 200 metres backstroke.

Walking

The *General household survey* showed that walking is the most popular UK sporting activity. The report stated that "41 per cent of all adults said that they had gone for a walk (of two miles or more) in the previous four weeks." So now we know the obvious: that, unlike most exercises, walking appears to be popular with all age groups and both sexes.

It is widely recognised that regular, brisk walking reduces blood pressure and keeps it down. This is because it encourages the production of the beneficial HDL (high density lipoprotein) cholesterol in the blood while reducing the level of the fatty cholesterol that is linked to heart disease.

According to the British Heart Foundation, regular walking is a low risk exercise that can also help to control weight, tone muscles, and avert aching joints and potential bone problems such as osteoporosis (brittle bones). If you have walked to the nearest village shop or pub every weekend for the last five years, you might feel like going further afield. The most useful organisation to approach for advice about walking in the countryside is the Ramblers Association. With over 100,000 members and more than 800 local organisations affiliated to the RA, the Association is well placed to provide information on country footpaths.

The Ramblers Association   **Tel: 0171-582 6878**
1/5 Wandsworth Road, London SW8 2XX

50 PLUS: STAYING FIT

T'ai Chi

Remember that slow-motion kung-fu-type dance you saw performed in a park? This form of Chinese exercise is very popular. There are many different aspects of T'ai Chi and it can be used effectively for health and healing. The exercises can be particularly useful in improving balance and physical co-ordination. As there is no national governing body solely devoted to T'ai Chi, the best way to find your nearest T'ai Chi teacher is to check in your local library or write to:

The British Council of Chinese Martial Arts
46 Oaston Road, Nuneaton, Warwickshire CV11 6JZ

Yoga

Yoga uses gentle and precise physical movement to develop suppleness, and breathing exercises to promote relaxation and meditation. Yoga can help to alleviate stress and anxiety, reduce blood pressure, and improve joint movement. According to a recent survey, movement of the shoulders in particular is significantly limited in those aged between 65 and 74, with about 17 per cent of those questioned unable to raise their arms more than 30 degrees above the horizontal. The back, neck and shoulders are especially prone to such stiffness but should be exercised only with great care. Some yoga exercises unnecessarily demand a degree of joint flexibility which is greater than that needed for normal use. Hyperextension of joints can damage them and prove both painful and disabling. There are no health benefits to be gained from unusual suppleness. A major additional benefit of yoga is that once the exercises have been mastered you can continue to practice them at home without further professional help.

British Wheel of Yoga   **Tel: 01529- 306 851**
1 Hamilton Place, Boston Road
Sleaford, Lincolnshire NG34 7ES

Special cases

The following organisations are useful contacts for older or disabled people:

British Sports Assocation for the Disabled   **Tel: 0171-490 4919**
The Mary Glen Haig Suite, Solecast House
13-27 Brunswick Place, London N1 6DX

Exercise Training for the Elderly and/or Disabled   **Tel: 0582-832 760**
22 Maltings Drive, Wheathampstead, Herts AL4 8QJ

EXTEND provides tapes and books of exercises which can be done to music in a limited space. It also has a national network of teachers trained to take classes.

5

Organisations that help

In this chapter we list the organisations which try to better your lot as you get older. Where these offer specific services or deal with specific problems, they are described in more detail in the relevant chapter.

Words or deeds?

There is a plethora of organisations which help older people, but their methods of doing it are changing. More charities appear happy to provide helpful advice but fewer to give actual financial or practical help. And sadly recession and the cult of individualism have taken their toll on charitable donations in the 1990s. While the National Lottery is raising vast amounts of money for distribution to charities, fewer people are giving privately. Financially, many charities dealing with the elderly already depend heavily on national grants or commercial agreements with local authorities to keep them afloat.

Technology, however, is making 'oldie' organisations more accessible: a mass of information, advice and counselling is often no further away than the end of a telephone helpline.

ORGANISATIONS THAT HELP

The organisations that offer direct practical help—usually a service like meals-on-wheels—are often the registered charities. Those which provide money in the form of a pension, grant or some other payment include benevolent funds.

Other organisations that are directly involved include self-help groups working at national or local level, where particular groups of people can tackle problems or undertake projects together.

Among those playing an indirect role are organisations carrying out research; for example, the charities funding medical research into diseases that commonly affect older people. Others act as advisory or pressure groups, often lobbying the government and influential policy formers to draw attention to problems for this age group and campaign for changes in the law. Some organisations combine several of these functions, such as the two British charities Age Concern and Help the Aged.

OLDIE ORGANISATIONS: DEFINITIONS

Registered charity.
There are some 170,000 of these in the UK, and all the types of organisations listed below can be charities. Many charities are multi-functional.

Benevolent fund.
A fund that gives financial help to categories of people it represents. Example: The Timber Trades Benevolent Society.

Pressure group
Think tank, policy unit or other organisation that campaigns on behalf of older people. May also carry out other functions: Example: Carers National Association.

Research body
An organisation that spends most of its funds on research into social or medical conditions affecting older people. Example: Research into Ageing.

Cooperative organisation
An organisation that helps people to help themselves or form networks for particular activities.
Example: University of the Third Age

ORGANISATIONS THAT HELP

Commercial organisations

Charities are usually dedicated, helpful and genuine in their aims. Sometimes, however, they are incompetent and fail to live up to professional standards. And just as in other fields, there are some commercial organisations which may present themselves as sources of unfailing goodness while being concerned purely with profit. A nursing home, for example, may use the name 'foundation' in its name where it is in fact a profit-making limited company. Knowing an organisation's reputation is essential.

National organisations

Not included in the list below are many charities which concern themselves with the welfare of particular groups, usually in the form of a benevolent fund associated with a trade, profession or industry. It is always worth checking out these bodies, because if you belong to a trade union or professional association, or if the company you worked for operates a hardship fund for former employees, you may be eligible for financial help in later years.

Benevolent funds and charities in these specialist areas range from the Actor's Charitable Trust to the Timber Trades Benevolent Society. These and company benevolent schemes sometimes extend to widows (and perhaps widowers), and can help, for example, with top-up funding for residential or nursing home costs. Some, like the Freemasons, even own nursing homes of their own. Benevolent funds may also offer other services such as counselling and advice or welfare visits.

•**Where to look:** The *Charities Digest* is probably the best source of information. Your local library should have a reference copy. *The Henderson Top 2000 Charities* directory lists benevolent funds in its 'Index of Expenditure Classification' under 'Welfare of Special Groups'. Or contact Charity Search, a free advisory service (see entry in listing).

Local organisations

There are a surprising number of small voluntary organisations providing services or programmes for elderly people which

ORGANISATIONS THAT HELP

operate only in a local area, especially in large cities. They may provide services ranging from repair or befriending schemes to active leisure projects. Many local Volunteer Bureaux provide a Help Service for one-off jobs such as driving someone to a hospital appointment or the occasional shopping.

•**Where to look:** your local council's information office or its officer in the social services department who deals with resources for the elderly should be able to provide you with a list of the voluntary organisations and charities operating in your area. Age Concern's *Senior Line* or your local Age Concern branch may also be able to help.

National organisations

The charities and other bodies listed below have some national representation. They will all do their best to help. You may already have supported their work with donations.

THE ABBEYFIELD SOCIETY

The Abbeyfield Society   **Tel: 01727-857 536**
(National Office) Abbeyfield House
53 Victoria Street, St Albans, Herts. AL1 3U

Abbeyfield Societies provide sheltered housing in 'supportive homes'. *See Chapter 10: Homes.*

AGE CONCERN

The largest of the charities working with older people, Age Concern operates nationally and locally through over 1,400 independent organisations:

Age Concern England   **Tel: 0181-679 8000**
Astral House, 1268 London Road, London SW16 4ER

Age Concern Scotland   **Tel: 0131-228 5656**
54a Fountainbridge, Edinburgh EH3 9PT

ORGANISATIONS THAT HELP

Age Concern Wales   **Tel: 01222-371 566**
4th Floor, 1 Cathedral Road, Cardiff CF1 9SD

Age Concern Northern Ireland   **Tel: 01232-245 729**
3 Lower Crescent, Belfast BT7 1NR

Age Concern promotes choice and opportunities for older people through research, by influencing and developing public policies and by operating training schemes for workers caring for elderly people. On a practical level it provides a wide range of services, support and advice.

•**How Age Concern can help:** services include a will-writing service, a funeral planning service (through Chosen Heritage, a commercial company, part of the controversial US company SCI), its own insurance policies and financial planning advice. Their emergency response service is a home alarm system linked to a 24-hour monitoring centre. Factsheets are available (up to five free if you send a large SAE) as is an excellent selection of information and advice books. Local Age Concern branches can give details of the programmes, services and facilities available in your area.

ALZHEIMER'S DISEASE SOCIETY

Alzheimer's Disease Society   **Tel: 0171-306 0606**
(England & Scotland) Gordon House
10 Greencoat Place, London SW1P 1PH

Information and advice, support through local branches, a range of publications including information and advice sheets. *See Chapter 11: Medical care.*

ANCHOR

Anchor   **Tel: 01865-311 511**
(Central Office) 269a Banbury Road
Oxford OX2 7HU

ORGANISATIONS THAT HELP

Anchor is the largest provider of non-profit making housing and care services for older people in the country and has developed many projects in partnership with local authorities. Research and informing and influencing decision-makers and resource-providers are also important elements of Anchor's work.

•**How Anchor can help:** Through the **Anchor Housing Association** it operates 650 sheltered housing schemes for rent, as well as operating residential and nursing homes. Another part of the Anchor Group, the **Guardian Housing Association,** develops and manages sheltered housing units for sale (*see Chapter 10*). Anchor's *staying put* service helps people who would like to stay in their own homes, where their flats or houses need to be repaired or adapted (*see Chapter 9: Surviving at home*).

ARTHRITIS AND RHEUMATISM COUNCIL (ARC)

The Arthritis and Rheumatism Council (ARC)   Tel: 01246-558 033
Copeman House, St Mary's Court
St Mary's Gate, Chesterfield, Derbyshire S41 7TD

Primarily a charity which funds research, ARC also produces over 40 free infomation booklets and leaflets and two videos. *See Chapter 11: Medical care.*

ARTHRITIS CARE

Arthritis Care   Tel: 0171-916 1500
18 Stephenson Way, London NW1 2HD

A voluntary organisation for arthritis sufferers. See Chapter 11.

ASSOCIATION OF RETIRED PEOPLE (ARP)

Association of Retired People (ARP Over 50)   Tel: 0171 828 0500
Greencoat House, Francis Street, London SW1P 1DZ.

ARP Over 50 is a self-help organisation whose aim is to represent the over 50s in Britain. Through advocacy, research, information programmes, and community services it supports its 120,000 members. Its also undertakes selective litigation against age discrimination and pension-related cases.

BACUP

The British Association of Cancer United Patients Tel: 0171-696 9003
3 Bath Place, Rivington Street, London EC2A 3JR

A nationwide cancer information service, cancer counselling service and a range of booklets on cancer. *See Chapter 11.*

BRITISH FEDERATION OF HOME CARE PROPRIETORS

The British Federation of Care Home Proprietors Tel: 0533-640 095
852 Melton Road, Thurmaston, Leicester LE4 8BNT

This is a trade body representing the owners of residential care homes. *See Chapter 10: Homes.*

BRITISH DIABETIC ASSOCIATION

The British Diabetic Association (BDA)   Tel: 0171-323 1531
10 Queen Anne Street, London W1M 0BD

The BDA has over 400 local branches and provides a confidential Care Line, publications and videos. *See Chapter 11: Medical care.*

BRITISH HEART FOUNDATION

The British Heart Foundation   Tel: 0171-935 0185
14 Fitzhardinge Street, London WC1H 4DH

The BHF provides leaflets and videos on all aspects of heart disease, including what to do if someone appears to be having a heart attack. *See Chapter 11: Medical care.*

ORGANISATIONS THAT HELP

BRITISH RED CROSS SOCIETY

The British Red Cross Society   **Tel: 0171-235 5454**
9 Grosvenor Crescent, London SW1X 7EE

Known for, among other things, the ambulances and nurses you
see at open-air festivals. The Red Cross operates a range of
nationwide services. In addition, local branches tailor their programmes to meet the needs of their community. Among them are
residential care homes and day centres for the elderly as well as
a holiday scheme where trained volunteers help frail older people on a one-to-one basis. You should be able to find details of
your local branch in the telephone directory, or contact national
headquarters at the address above.
• **How the Red Cross can help:** the *medical loan service* lends
equipment such as wheelchairs or bath seats, while the *home from
hospital* scheme provides trained volunteers who give support to
patients (and their carers) for up to four weeks after they leave
hospital. The *transport and escort service* is available for anyone
who finds it difficult to travel.

CANCERLINK

CancerLink   **Tel: 0171-833 2818**
17 Britannia Street, London WC1X 9JN

CancerLink in Scotland   **Tel: 0131-228 5567**
9 Castle Terrace, Edinburgh EH1 2DP

CancerLink provides an information line, factsheets, audio tapes
and videos, and information on local self-help and support
groups. *See Chapter 11: Medical Care.*

CARERS NATIONAL ASSOCIATION

Carers National Association (England)   **Tel: 0171-490 8818**
Ruth Pitter House   Carers Line: 0171-490 8898
20-25 Glasshouse Yard, London EC1A 4JS

Carers National Association (Scotland)   **Tel: 0141-333 9495**
11 Queen's Crescent, Glasgow G4 9AS

The Carers National Association does not offer direct practical help. Its offices—manned by serious-minded people who in 1995 were trying to get a new Bill (The Carers Bill) through parliament—is a pressure group which campaigns for better services and policies for carers, usually people who devote most of their time to looking after a dependent relative. It has a network of regional offices and 150 local support groups run by volunteers. Ring national offices to find out about your local group. *See Chapter 8: Community care.*
•**How Carers National Association can help:** There is a Carers Line which gives information and advice to carers. CNA also publishes a series of free factsheets and leaflets.

CENTRE FOR POLICY ON AGEING

Centre for Policy on Ageing (CPA)   **Tel: 0171-253 1787**
25-31 Ironmonger Row, London EC1V 3QP

The CPA develops policy on a wide range of issues about older people and publishes its findings, which are also covered by the media. It also holds conferences and exhibitions and encourages a 'positive redefinition' of older people as an under-used resource in society. As well as its main work, the centre runs an information service and a library, which it describes as Britain's foremost documentation centre on the social and behavioural aspects of ageing. Visits by appointment only.

CHARITY SEARCH

Charity Search   **Tel: 0117-982 4060**
25 Portview Road, Avonmouth, Bristol, BS 11 9LD

This is a registered charity which will help you find the charity (or charities) which can give financial help for your particular

ORGANISATIONS THAT HELP

need. It is a free service that specializes in giving advice to elderly people and will help as much as it can: for example, by going through a grant application form with you.

CITIZENS ADVICE BUREAU

National Association of Citizens   **Tel: 0171-833 2181**
  Advice Bureaux (NACAB)
115-123 Pentonville Road, London N1 9LZ

A first stop for advice on almost any subject relating to daily life—but you could tuck a novel under your arm, because there is often a long wait. The network of 750 Citizens Advice Bureaux throughout the UK employs an army of volunteers and can help with free information. If the CAB is not able to help it should be able to tell you who can.
•**Where to look:** For your local Citizens Advice Bureau look in the telephone directory or contact the National Association of Citizens Advice Bureaux.

COUNSEL AND CARE

Counsel and Care   **Tel: 0171-485 1550**
Twyman House   Advice Line: 0171-485 1566
16 Bonny Street, London NW1 9PG   (10.30am-4.00pm)

Counsel and Care has been giving advice and help to the elderly and their carers since 1954. As well as giving practical help, it campaigns vigorously on behalf of older people, focusing on services, care and quality of life through research, policy development, conferences and publications.
•**How Counsel and Care can help:** *See Chapter 10: Homes.*

COUNTRY COUSINS EMPLOYMENT BUREAU

Country Cousins   **Tel: 01403-210 415**
10 A Market Square, Horsham, W. Sussex RH12 1EX

ORGANISATIONS THAT HELP

Country Cousins supplies temporary residential helpers, many of whom have nursing or care home backgrounds, for the general care of people during convalescence or illness. They cover all areas of the country, even the far north of Scotland, as helpers are found locally.

CROSSROADS CARE
(Association of Crossroads Care Attendant Schemes)

Crossroads Care (England)	**Tel: 01788-573 653**
10 Regent Place, Rugby	
Warwickshire CV21 2PN	
Crossroads Care (Scotland)	**Tel: 0141-226 3793**
24 George Square, Glasgow G2 1EG	
Crossroads Care (Wales)	**Tel: 01222-222 282**
Unit 5, Cooper's Yard,	
Curran Road, Cardiff CF1 5DF	

Crossroads is a well-known charity offering practical help to carers. It runs schemes to try to relieve the stresses felt by carers by providing a community-based respite service . It has 10 regional offices and over 237 local schemes. You may be referred to a Crossroads unit by your social services department, but you can find details of schemes in your area by contacting the addresses above.

• **How Crossroads can help:** local Crossroads units will send a trained care attendant (whose services are free) to relieve carers through both regular and occasional visits. Both day and overnight visits can be arranged. Crossroads aims to provide a regular care attendant who will take over all the work a carer would normally be doing. Even if a carer or person being cared for is already receiving visits from a community care worker or other help, visits from Crossroads can usually still be arranged. In some schemes a carer support worker is available for information and advice. *See Chapter 8: Social Services*

ORGANISATIONS THAT HELP

CRUSE

Cruse Bereavement Care Ltd   **Tel: 0181-940 4818**
126 Sheen Road   Bereavement Line: 0181-332 7227
Richmond, Surrey TW9 1UR   Mon-Fri 9.30 - 5.00

Cruse is the largest bereavement counselling organisation of its type in the world, with nearly 200 local branches and over 6,000 volunteers. It offers a nationwide service of counselling, information and social support for those who have been bereaved. It has 65 drop-in centres throughout the UK where bereaved people can call without an appointment. Details of your nearest branch can be obtained from Cruse headquarters. Those who do not have a branch nearby can become national members of Cruse. *(See also Chapter 13)*

•**How Cruse can help:** local branches have counsellors available to visit in the home or elsewhere, regular social meetiings for the widowed, and can give advice on practical matters through specialists or Cruse publications. National members can receive counselling and advice through letters or over the phone (see the **Bereavement Line** above). A contact list enables widowed national members to get in touch with other national members. All members receive the *Cruse Chronicle*. Cruse publications (please send sae for list) include leaflets and books on bereavement and fact sheets on practical matters.

DGAA HOMELIFE

DGAA Homelife   **Tel: 0171-396 6700**
(The Distressed Gentlefolk's Aid Association)
1 Derry Street, London W8 5HY

The DGAA understandably doesn't lay down rules about what makes someone a gentleperson—it only states that you must come from a professional or similar background. The photos in its newsletter exude heritage, embroidery, bridge, gardens, good wine and other fairly civilised interests. They try to assist people to stay in their own homes as long as possible. DGAA also has a

54

sheltered housing scheme and operates residential care and nursing homes.

ELDERLY ACCOMMODATION COUNCIL

Elderly Accommodation Council　　　　　**Tel: 0181-995 8320**
46A Chiswick High Road, London W4 1SZ

The Elderly Accommodation Council aims to provide easily accessible information to elderly people seeking suitable accommodation. Its computerised national register covers all types of accommodation in the charity, private and local authority sectors, including retirement housing (sheltered and independent, for rent and for sale), Abbeyfield-style accommodation, almshouses, residential care homes, nursing homes and terminal hospices.

•**How the Elderly Accommodation Council can help:** EAC operates an information service on the types of accommodation listed above and an advice service on sources of TOP-UP FUNDING for care costs. The accommodation service matches the enquirer's requirements and eligibility for accommodation available in the area in which they wish to live. It does not place people or recommend establishments. A small search fee is requested for both services, though this is waived for those on low incomes. The introductory booklet *For you and yours* includes application forms for each service. Two leaflets, *Looking for retirement housing?* and *Choosing the right home* are also available free.

HELP THE AGED

Help the Aged　　　　　　　**Tel: 0171-253 0253**
St James's Walk,　　　　　　　SeniorLine: 0800-289 404
Clerkenwell Green　　　　　　　(Minicom: 0800-269 626)
London EC1R 0BE

Help the Aged is a big national charity that, by identifying needs, campaigning and fundraising, hopes to improve the quality of

ORGANISATIONS THAT HELP

life for elderly people, particularly those who are frail, isolated or poor, both in the UK and internationally. Though Help the Aged describes itself as an 'enabling' organisation, by for instance, donating minibuses to local groups and funding day centres, it also provides advice and practical help directly to older people.

•**How Help the Aged can help:** *SeniorLine* is its free national information service which gives advice on welfare and disability benefits, housing, health, support for carers, mobility, community alarms, wills, sources of local practical help and other voluntary organisations (number and times above). It also operate a *Winter warmth advice line* (dial the *SeniorLine* number), which is part of the Department of Health's 'Keep Warm Keep Well' campaign. Free advice leaflets on money-related, health-related and home safety subjects are available from the information department (with 9"x 6" SAE), as is a *Will information pack.* from the Wills and legacies department. The *Community alarm programme* provides personal alarm systems linked by telephone to 24-hour control centres which will arrange for emergency assistance when alerted. Under the *Gifted housing plan* elderly people can donate their house to Help the Aged, who take over responsibility for the property while allowing the resident to remain living there or to move to one of Help the Aged's sheltered properties. As well as running a large number of semi-sheltered and extra-sheltered accomodation schemes, Help the Aged also operates five residential care homes.

INDEPENDENT HEALTHCARE ASSOCIATION

The Independent Healthcare Association   **Tel: 071-430 0537**
22 Little Russell Street, London WC1A 2HT

A trade association that represents.the majority of the UK's independent health care providers. Its members include independent acute and psychiatric hospitals, nursing and residential care homes, screening units and day surgeries. The Association can provide prospective care home residents with a local list of homes which are members of the IHA, or a full breakdown of

ORGANISATIONS THAT HELP

IHA-affiliated homes throughout the UK. However, the Association points out that a home's inclusion in its list is not a recommendation. *See Chapter 10: Homes.*

MENCAP

MENCAP (Royal Society for Mentally   **Tel: 0171-454 0454**
  Handicapped Children and Adults)
123 Golden Lane, London EC1Y 0RT

MENCAP provides a wide range of services for people with learning disabilities and their carers.

MIND

MIND (National Association for Mental Health) **Tel: 0181-519 2122**
Granta House, 15-19   Info Line: 0181-522 1728
The Broadway, Stratford, London E15 4BQ

With over 240 local associations, MIND is the leading mental health charity in England and Wales. It gives advice, support and information (including a range of publications) for those with mental health problems and their carers.

NATIONAL ASSOCIATION OF WIDOWS

National Association of Widows   **Tel: 0121-643 8348**
54-57 Allison Street, Digbeth, Birmingham, B5 5TH

A support group providing information and advice with a network of about 70 local self-help groups. The national office (address above) can tell you if there is a group in your area or help you to set one up.

ORGANISATIONS THAT HELP

NATIONAL BENEVOLENT FUND FOR THE AGED

National Benevolent Fund for the Aged (NBFA)   Tel: 0181-688 6655
1 Leslie Grove Place , Croydon CRO 6TJ

NBFA provides group holidays for self-sufficient people over 65 who are receiving income support, housing benefit or council tax benefit and who have not had a holiday for at least five years. However, this last condition of eligibility can be waived in the case of recent illness or bereavement.

NURSING AGENCIES *See Chapter 11, Medical Care.*

NATIONAL OSTEOPOROSIS SOCIETY

The National Osteoporosis Society   Tel: 01761-432 472
PO Box 10, Radstock, Bath BA3 3BY

An association that helps sufferers from the brittle-bone syndrome known as osteoporosis. *See Chapter 11: Medical care.*

OFFICER'S ASSOCIATION

Royal British Legion   Tel: 0171-930 0125
(Officer's Association)   Tel: 0171-973 0633
48 Pall Mall, London SW1Y 5JY

Royal British Legion (Scotland)   Tel: 0131-557 2782
New Haig House, Logie Green Road,
Edinburgh EH7 4HR

The officers' benevolent department of the Royal British Legion supports ex-servicemen, their widows and dependents, and can help with claims for war pensions and hardship grants.

ORGANISATIONS THAT HELP

THE PARKINSON'S DISEASE SOCIETY

The Parkinson's Disease Society (PDS)   **Tel: 0171-383 3513**
22 Upper Woburn Place, London WC1H 0RA

Like the Alzheimer's Disease Society, the PDS is an association representing people with a specific illness. It provides a *helpline*, publications (many free of charge) and a network of local branches or self-help support groups. *See Chapter 11: Medical care.*

PRE-RETIREMENT ASSOCIATION

Pre-Retirement Association (PRA)   **Tel: 01483-301 170**
26 Fredericks Hanger Road, Research Park,
Guildford GU2 5YD

The PRA is primarily a trainer of trainers for pre-retirement courses, but it runs courses for people coming up to retirement , showing them how to use their time constructively. Its resource centre is the main source for retirement information. There are around 30 affiliated Active Retirement Associations around the country which organise retirement activities.

RADAR

RADAR (The Royal Association for   **Tel: 0171-250 3222**
   Disability and Rehabilitation)   Minicom: 0171-250 4119
12 City Forum, 250 City Road
London EC1V 8AF

A national campaigning organisation for disabled people.
•**How RADAR can help:** their information department gives advice on all aspects of disability as well as support to those trying to obtain services. It also coordinates the *national key* scheme for independent entrance to accessible public lavatories. Publications list.

ORGANISATIONS THAT HELP

REACH

Reach   **Tel: 0171-928 0452**
27 Bankside, London SE1 9DP

This charity runs a service for retired professionals and executives over 65 who would like to continue useful work. Run by people who are themselves over 65, it places older people in jobs with registered charities where they can use their skills and experience (for example as former accountants, lawyers or managers). Work is unpaid. In 1994 Reach placed 600 people in work with charities. *See also Chapter 6: Staying busy.*

•**How Reach can help:** You can apply to Reach as a retired 65+ professional looking for unpaid or useful work. Or, if you are an older person already helping to run a charity, you can contact Reach when you need to recruit staff with specific expertise.

RESEARCH INTO AGEING

Research into Ageing   **Tel: 0171-404 6878**
Baird House, 15-17 St Cross Street
London EC1N 8UN

Research into Ageing funds pioneering clinical and scientific research into the medical conditions which affect old age, with the underlying philosophy of improving the health and quality of life of older people. Research into Ageing-funded projects have achieved success in such areas as dementia, osteoporosis, drug metabolism and wound-healing.

•**How Research into Ageing can help:** Research into Ageing publishes a series of informative free leaflets on dementia, osteoporosis, urinary incontinence, exercise and visual problems in old age. A booklet on safe exercise regimes for the elderly is also available.

ORGANISATIONS THAT HELP

RELATIVES ASSOCIATION

Relatives Association   **Tel: 0171-916 6055**
Tavistock Place, London WC1H 9SS

The Relatives Association helps the relatives and friends of elderly people who are going into or already living in a residential care or nursing home. The Association can give advice on all aspects of the care system, from the assessment process to property problems. They campaign actively on issues and legislation which affect residential care and nursing home residents and their relatives and friends. There are around 15 local relatives groups, some organised through other organisations such as Age Concern. Call the number above for the location of the group nearest you.

RNIB

Royal National Institute for the Blind   **Tel: 0171-388 1266**
224 Great Portland Street, London W1N 6AA

RNIB provides services for the partially-sighted (visually-impaired) as well as the blind. *See Chapter 11: Medical care.*

RNID

Royal National Institute for Deaf People   **Tel: 0171-387 8033**
10 Gower Street, London WC1E 6AH

RNID provides a range of services for deaf people including 'Sound Advantage' which markets helpful hearing assistive devices. *See Chapter 11: Medical care.*

STROKE ASSOCIATION

The Stroke Association   **Tel: 0171-490 2686**
CHSA House, Whitecross Street, London EC1Y 8JJ

ORGANISATIONS THAT HELP

This association has information centres which provide helplines, publications, one-off welfare grants and *family support* and *dyphasic support* programmes. *See Chapter 11: Medical care.*

UNITED KINGDOM HOME CARE ASSOCIATION

United Kingdom Home Care Association   **Tel: 0222-473 954**
22 Southway, Carshalton, Surrey SM5 4HWT

UKHCA will provide information about domiciliary care (home help) agencies in your area.

WOMEN'S ROYAL VOLUNTARY SERVICE (WRVS)

Women's Royal Voluntary Service (WRVS)   **Tel: 0171-416 0146**
234-244 Stockwell Road, London SW9 9SP

If the initials WRVS make you think of Vera Lynn, woolly socks and steaming gravy, it's probably because it's the UK's largest voluntary organisation and famed for its meals on wheels (15 million delivered annually). The WRVS provides a variety of services for the elderly including residential care homes, day centres, luncheon clubs and a holiday scheme. In hospitals WRVS volunteers help with extra care for patients—from hairdressing to letter-writing. Services will differ at each branch. Look in the phone book for your local branch or contact WRVS head office at the address above.
•**How the WRVS can help:** *Meals with care* is a home-delivered frozen meals service. *Books on wheels* delivers library books to your home, while *home support* volunteers will help you with practical tasks like collecting prescriptions. WRVS also runs a transport scheme.

65 to 100: Staying busy

Will you just potter round the garden when you retire? To some people the idea of having nothing much to do is bliss, to others dull. There is also the strong possibility, in these uncertain times, that you may find yourself having to continue to earn some money to keep you afloat. So this section looks at both paid and voluntary work, followed by a few amusements.

Paid work

No-one needs telling that paid work is scarce for people who admit to being over 65. Often the difficulty starts at 50. For professionals however (for example accountants, architects, solicitors) computers are making it easier to carry on working beyond official retirement. No longer does the golden oldie need a smart office with a secretary to do some consulting: a room can be manned with a few machines. Anyone with experience, imagination and contacts can continue their occupation in a modest

65 PLUS: STAYING BUSY

way. For those who have spent most of their lives bringing up a family and now want to do something different, it is worth getting well-informed about career moves first. Beware of expensive retraining courses which promise a 'new start': a course organiser or college should always be asked for concrete evidence that people who have completed its course have found the paid work they want afterwards.

Employment tax

People over the age of 65 are allowed a higher than standard personal allowance, the *age allowance*, before they start having to pay tax. Although this is a tax advantage mainly designed to let people enjoy more of their interest and dividend income from sav-

---

INCOME TAX 1995/6

Personal allowance (to age 65)	£3,525
Married couple's allowance (to age 65)	*£1,720
Age allowance (65-74)§	
Personal allowance	£4,630
Married couple's allowance	*£2,995
Age allowance (75 or over)§	
Personal allowance	£4,800
Married couple's allowance	*£3,035
Income limit for age allowance	£14,600

*Relief restricted to 15% for 1995/6. §If total income, less allowable deductions, of a taxpayer aged 65 or over exceeds the income limit, the age-related allowances are reduced by £1 for each additional £2 of income until the basic levels of the personal or married couple allowances are reached.

Cheltenham & Gloucester Building Society

---

ings in retirement than they have been able to during their working lives, it is also encouraging for over-65s who want to carry on earning a modest living. In the tax year 1995/6, after the tax-free allowance, you would have had to pay 20 per cent tax on the next £3,200 of income, with the rate rising to 25 per cent from £3,201 to £24,300 and 40 per cent above £24,300.

Voluntary work

For anyone with time to do voluntary work, there is a wealth of choice. Most charities will welcome volunteers of any age with open arms. Your local Volunteer Bureau should be able to direct you to the organisation most suitable for you.

It might be worth trying for an advisory job, for example, at a local Citizen's Advice Bureau (CAB). The CAB is happy to employ volunteers who can master and explain citizen's rights to the public in a simple way. The London region alone has 120 branches: aspiring volunteers should call the London head office (136 City Road, London EC1V 2QN. Tel: 0171-251 2000) to arrange an appointment. An application form has to be filled in at this meeting.

Many of the charities listed in Chapter 5 employ volunteers, and for anyone who would like to help a fellow oldie by, for example, delivering meals-on-wheels, charities like WRVS are an obvious choice. Head office numbers are listed in Chapter 5, but volunteers are usually asked to contact their local branch.

There is also an agency, REACH, which specialises in placing retired professionals or experienced businessmen and women with registered charities:

REACH

Retired Executive Action Clearing House   **Tel: 0171-928 0452**
27 Bankside, London SE1 9DP

REACH stands for Retired Executive Action Clearing House, (although they don't like the term 'executive' because it sounds exclusive). It can place all types of retired people with professional qualifications or experience, including business people,

BUSINESS ANGELS

If you have retired with some spare capital and sound business sense and you can't shake off the itch to take risks, you could subscribe to one of the publications or networks that puts you in touch with small businesses looking for minority shareholders who can also lend their expertise. These include:

Capital Exchange	Tel: 01432 342 484
Linc	Tel: 0171-236 3000
Venturenet	Tel: 01483 458 111

High Court judges, civil servants, engineers or teachers. Reach is itself a registered charity and the placements that it offers are voluntary part-time posts within other charities, the majority of which are also registered. People tend to join Reach if they have retired or have been made redundant and feel that they still have a lot to offer as a result of their years of experience in their particular fields.

The age range of the volunteers is between 27 and over 80, the average age is 60 and they are placed in a variety of jobs such in large or small charities involved with, for example, caring, health, enviroment, arts or heritage. They are placed locally for easy access and for one to three days a week.

•*Useful reading* Jobs After 50 by Linda Greenbury, Piatkus.

Trivial pursuits

Here are some useful addresses for a few of many pursuits for people lucky enough to have time on their hands: education, gardening, holidays and travel, music and talking books.

Education

Keeping the intellect alive can be done with a university degree as the goal or for no greater end in mind than the enjoyment of Roman remains. Serious thinkers who can still write analytically and sit rigorous exams can either contact a local university to ask about admissions for mature students or apply to the Open University, a vast 'campus'network with a wonderfully mixed bag of students:

65 PLUS: STAYING BUSY

OPEN UNIVERSITY

The Open University   **Tel: 01908-653 231**
Central Enquiry Service, PO Box 200
Milton Keynes MK7 6YZ

The OU offers a very wide range of courses, from 'interest only' to post-graduate research. Students go at their own pace and tutors are always available for guidance by telephone. There are no entrance requirements for undergraduates and associate level courses. People who can't keep up to exacting standards tend to drop out in the first few weeks.

NATIONAL EXTENSION COLLEGE

The National Extension College   **Tel: 01223-316 644**
18 Brooklands Avenue, Cambridge, CB2 2HN

Offers correspondence courses related to leisure, health, business, languages and returning to study, as well as traditional academic subjects.

OPEN COLLEGE OF ARTS

The Open College of Arts   **Tel: 01226-730 495**
Hound Hill, Worsbrough Barnsley,
South Yorkshire S70 6TU

Not connected with the Open University. Offers courses in art and design, painting, sculpture, photography, writing and music. Students have to attend ten tutorials throughout the year. Course fees range from £195 to £250.

UNIVERSITY OF THE THIRD AGE

The University of the Third Age (U3A)   **Tel: 0171- 737 2541**
Third Age Trust, 1 Stockwell Green, London SW9 9JF

U3A, which consists of about 260 groups throughout the UK, is run specifically for and by older people. No qualifications are

65 PLUS: STAYING BUSY

needed to take part and none are given, as each group draws on the experiences and skills of its own members and decides on its own study plan and activities. Each group is responsible for its funding and a small subscription enables most groups to fund themselves. A pack is available for those interested in starting their own groups. The Third Age Trust, the charity which is the national representative body of the U3A movement in the UK, helps to promote and develop new groups and provides services such as *Third Age News*, published three times a year.

Gardening

Mainstay of oldie life. If Great-Aunt Annie isn't already a member of the Royal Horticultural Society a membership makes a wonderful present. If she has a knee operation that fails and she can no longer bend her right leg to reach the *Herbespeciosa* there is also an organisation that helps:

ROYAL HORTICULTURAL SOCIETY

Royal Horticultural Society   **Tel: 0171-834 4333**
80 Vincent Square, London SW1P 2PB

Becoming a member of the Royal Horticultural Society will give you free entry to gardens across the country, free advice on your gardening problems, a monthly magazine and privileged entry to the Chelsea Flower Show and other gardening fairs.

65 PLUS: STAYING BUSY

NATIONAL TRUST

National Trust   **Tel: 0171-222 9251**
36 Queen Anne's Gate, London SW1H 9AS

National Trust for Scotland   **Tel: 0131-226 5922**
5 Charlotte Square, Edinburgh EH2 4DU

Almost too well-known to need explaining, membership of the National Trust gives you free entry into hundreds of NT properties and their gardens around the country.

GARDENS FOR THE DISABLED TRUST

Gardens for the Disabled Trust   **Tel: 0580-712 196**
Hayes Farmhouse, Hayes Lane, Peasmarsh
Rye, East Sussex, TN31 6XR

Provides advice on making gardens and gardening more accessible to people with any form of disability. The Trust runs a gardening club which publishes a quarterly newsletter

HORTICULTURAL THERAPY

Horticultural Therapy   **Tel: 01373-464 782**
Goulds Ground, Vallis Way
Frome, Somerset BA11 3DW

Provides information for gardeners with special needs and can advise on who to contact to arrange talks on gardening matters. Horticultural Therapy has some demonstration gardens at Battersea Park, Bunhill Field, Islington, and Trunkwell Park and Beach Hill in Reading.

65 PLUS: STAYING BUSY

Holidays and travel

For younger oldies, travel is not a problem: Incompatibility may be more likely to cause stress abroad than illness. When on holiday Great-Uncle Archie likes to tell strangers about his exploits in Aden, while Great-Aunt Annie repeats her Aldeburgh Festival performance as Lady Teazle, driving everyone else back to their hotel rooms. Is it surprising that as they get older couples often take separate holidays?

Whether oldies prefer to travel independently or as a couple, almost anything except a seriously athletic holiday goes. Audio guides and other aids, for example, have made visits to galleries and museums easier for people who find it exhausting to stand too long. Travel companies like SAGA specialise in package holidays for older people, but as long as the travel agency, organiser and the travel insurer are fully informed about any medical condition that may be a risk, there is no reason why an 80-something need not travel with a 30-something. There is no shortage of travel agencies that organise chaperoned tours of civilised parts of the world, often with academic experts to act as guides. Here (names supplied by ABTA marked with an asterisk) are a few tour operators which organise holidays for people over 50:

Airtours *   **Tel: 01706-240 033**
Wavell House, Holcombe Road
Helmshore, Rossendale, Lancs BB4 4NB

Bales Tours*   **Tel: 01306-885 991**
Bales House, Junction Road, Dorking, Surrey RH4 3H

Cosmosair * (Golden Times brochure)   **Tel: 0181-464 3444**
Tourama House, 17 Holmsdale Road
Bromley, Kent BR2 9LX

First Choice Holidays and Flights*   **Tel: 01293-560 777**
First Choice House, London Road
Crawley, West Sussex RH10 2GX

65 PLUS: STAYING BUSY

Kuoni*   **Tel: 0171-374 6601**
84 Bishopsgate, London EC2N 4AU

La France des Villages   **Tel: 01449-737 664**
(Self-catering, 'easily managed canal barges')
Model Farm, Rattlesden
Bury St Edmunds, Suffolk 1P30 05Y

SAGA (Only for over-50s)   **Tel: 01303-857 000**
Saga Building, Middleburg Square
Folkstone, Kent CT20 1AZ

Shearing Holidays*   **Tel: 01942-44246**
Miry Lane, Wigan, Lancs WN3 4AG

Solo's Holidays (for singles, 55+)   **Tel: 0181-202 0855**
41 Watford Way, London NW4 3JH

Sunworld* (Iberotravel Ltd)   **Tel: 0181-290 1111**
Devonshire House, 29-31 Elmfield Road
Bromley, Kent BR1 1LT

Swan Hellenic (cruises)   **Tel: 0171-800 2300**
77 New Oxford Street, London WC1A 1PP

Thomson Holidays* (Young at Heart)*   **Tel: 0171-387 9321**
Greater London House, Hampstead Road
London NW1 7SD

Wallace Arnold Tours*   **Tel: 0113-263 6456**
Gelderd Road, Leeds LS12 6DH

•*Useful reading* For anyone worried about holidays and travel who is looking for advice Age Concern England (Tel: 0181-679 8000) provides a useful fact sheet called *Holidays for older people.*

Holidays: special needs

Organisations which cater for older and/or disabled people include the British Sports Association for the Disabled *(see Chapter 4)* and National Benevolent Fund for the Aged *(see Chapter 5).*

65 PLUS: STAYING BUSY

THE HOLIDAY CARE SERVICE

Holiday Care Service   **Tel: 01293-774 535**
2 Old Bank Chambers   Minicom: 01293-776 943
Station Road, Horley, Surrey RH6 9HW

HCS is a charity which provides free information and advice on holidays for people with special needs, such as publications on accommodation, transport, possible sources of financial help, guides on package holidays in the UK and abroad, and information on specialised holidays organised by voluntary organisations. HCS also run a scheme called *holiday helpers*, which aims to introduce voluntary helpers to disabled or elderly people requiring a carer or a companion on an ordinary holiday.

THE WINGED FELLOWSHIP

Winged Fellowship   **Tel: 0171-833 2594**
Angel House, 20/32 Pentonville Road
London N1 9XD

Winged Fellowship has its own holiday centres designed and equipped for disabled people. Guests are cared for by permanent staff and volunteers and there is continuous nursing cover. The funding support officer can advise about possible help with the cost of the holiday.

Buses and coaches

If you qualify for a pension you may qualify also for a travel permit from your local authority. A travel permit entitles the holder to free or subsidised travel on public transport. However local authorities have to consider their individual financial constraints when issuing these permits. So although some local authorities may provide travel permits free of charge, others may ask you for a financial contribution to defray their costs. Travel permits can only be used after the morning rush hour.

Victoria Coach Station   Tel :0171-730 3466
National Express   Tel: 0171-730 0202

65 PLUS: STAYING BUSY

National Express, the UK coach operator, has a discount travel card scheme for the over 55s. A £7 card gives the holder a 30 per cent discount on coach fares for a year, and an £18 card gives the same discounts for 3 years. Do tell National Express about any travelling difficulties, as the company will complete a *customer assistance form* when taking your booking and make sure that staff are on hand to help.

Trains

British Rail publishes a leaflet called (*British Rail and the disabled traveller*) that gives information on making your journey, lists phone numbers of the local contact points able to arrange help for travellers, and includes an application form for a *disabled person's railcard*. Should you be eligible for one, the £14 railcard is valid for 12 months and allows discounts of up to a third off most BR services. Applications should be sent to: The Disabled Persons Railcard Office, PO Box, York YO1 1FB.

British Rail   **Tel: 01904-639 174**
British Railways Board, Euston House
24 Eversholt Street, London NW1 1DZ

Planes

Airlines prefer to know if there are any complications that may arise when travelling, whether due to a disability or a medical condition, the unit will ensure that any necessary help is provided. It is up to the person travelling to inform the unit of his or her requirements in advance, so that there is plenty of time to make the necessary arrangements. British Airways, for example, has a special telephone advice line:

British Airways   **Tel: 0181-562 7070**
Incapacitated Passenger Unit

Ships

The same rules apply: inform the tour operators of any special needs when making reservations.

65 PLUS: STAYING BUSY

Holidays: who looks after the house?

For many people, of any age, leaving a house that may become prey for burglars is a worry that can spoil a holiday. There are companies which will provide someone to live in your house while you are away who will water the plants and feed the cat. Staff are thoroughly vetted and tend to be retired service or security personnel.

Housewatch Ltd　　　　　　　　　　　**Tel: 01279-777 412**
Little London, Berdon,
Bishops Stortford, Herts CM23 1BE

Homesitters Ltd　　　　　　　　　　　**Tel: 01296-630 730**
Buckland Wharf, Buckland,
Aylesbury, Bucks HP22 5LQ

Music

Here are some organisations which help to keep music accessible for older people:

The National Music　　　　　　　　　　**Tel: 01803-866 701**
　and Disability Information Service
Dartington Hall, Totnes, Devon TQ9 6EB

This service offers ideas about the use of music in residential establishments, and can provide information, training, and details about large-print music and other resources.

The Council for Music in Hospitals　　　**Tel: 01932-252 809**
74 Queens Road, Hersham, Surrey KT12 5LW

The CMH organises as many as 3,000 concerts a year, given by professional musicians who will perform in any residential home no matter how small it is. If Great-Aunt Annie is in a home, it's worth lobbying for her favourite composers to be played.

65 PLUS: STAYING BUSY

Artsline   **Tel: 0171-388 2227**
5 Crowndale Road, London NW1 1TU

Artsline is an organisation for disabled people which lists information on courses, classes and workshops, and arts and entertainment events in London.

Tapes and talking books

Audio books or 'talking books' make wonderful presents for oldies. These tape recordings of classic novels, thrillers, racy blockbusters and other literary works are now available in most bookshops and the repertoire is constantly growing. They are hugely popular with different age groups—from 30-somethings driving to Tuscany to 70-somethings who can wear a walkman while weeding the garden. They are obviously particularly suitable for anyone who is blind or cannot read. And you can now get special earphones available for partly·deaf people to plug into a walkman to amplify the sound. Here are some addresses:

THE TALKING BOOK CLUB

11 Lettice Street   **Tel: 0171 731 6262**
London SW6 4EH

The Talking Book Club was one of the first independent talking book clubs, and by mid-1995 it had a about 1,300 members throughout the UK. The club has a library of over 2,000 books recorded on to tape that members can rent from for fees that start at a mere £1.25 a week. Membership of the club costs £7.50.

ROYAL NATIONAL INSTITUTE FOR THE BLIND

RNIB   **Tel: 0171-388 1266**
224 Great Portland Street, London W1N 6AA

The RNIB has a talking book service for those who cannot see to read, or those who find reading difficult for any other reason. It

65 PLUS: STAYING BUSY

DOG-EARED

When Zoë Richmond-Watson and Annie Muir open the door to welcome you into their converted glass works in Fulham, dogs leap from every corner. The two women started The Talking Book Club in 1989: chatting over a garden wall, they agreed that people like them didn't have enough time to read. Now they are surrounded by shelves stacked high with tapes, many of them unabridged recordings of long novels. By mid-1995 The Talking Book Club had 1,300 members, varying from lorry drivers to wrinklies. For the many older ones it is an important part of their lives. "One lady sends us a box of Belgian chocolates every Christmas from Wigan," says Muir. There is a pile of heart-warming letters on the desk and the two are always ready to chat to a borrower on the phone.

---

has a library of 6,500 tapes. Annual membership costs £47 (plus VAT if paid by a local authority). The tapes are played on special playback machines, which are provided free, and there is no charge for postage and packing. The RNIB express reading service can also record knitting patterns onto tape. It is worth contacting local groups for blind people to see if this service is available in your area. The RNIB can also provide modified board games to enable sighted and partially or non-sighted people to play together. Applications for membership should be made to:

The RNIB Talking Book Service   **Tel.: 0181-903 6666**
Mount Pleasant, Wembley, London HA0 1RR

TALKING NEWSPAPER ASSOCIATION

The Talking Newspaper Association   **Tel: 01435-866 102**
    of the UK
10 Browning Road, Heathfield, East Sussex TN21 8DB

Records magazines and newspapers onto tape. The Association charges a £15 annual membership fee, which allows the member to subscribe to as many recordings as they wish. There are also more than 500 groups covering local news items.

NATIONAL LISTENING LIBRARY

The National Listening Library (NLL)   **Tel: 0171-407 9417**
12 Lant Street, London SE1 1QH

The NLL provides machines and tape recordings of over 3,000 book titles and, as in the case of tapes from the RNIB, there's just a chance a local authority may pay the annual membership fee (currently £25). As the NLL caters specifically for those with non-sight disabilities, individuals applying for library membership need a medical practitioner or other recognised authority to confirm that they are disabled and would benefit from the library's services. Applications should be sent to the above address.

Games, puzzles, presents

Stuck for a present for someone whose eyesight, hearing or other faculties are failing? Here are a few ideas.

PARTIALLY SIGHTED SOCIETY

The Partially Sighted Society   **Tel: 01302-323 132**
PO Box 322, Doncaster, South Yorks, DN1 2XA

Produce large-print crosswords and playing cards.

WINSLOW PRESS

Winslow Press, Telford Road, Bicester   **Tel: 01869-244 733**
Oxfordshire, OX6 OTS

The Winslow Press makes large-piece versions of jigsaws, Snakes and Ladders, chess, draughts, Scrabble, and Ludo.

65 PLUS: STAYING BUSY

Reminiscence

Remembering the past and sharing our memories with others can be a creative and meaningful activity as we become older. Winslow Press (above) also publishes a book called *Reminiscence with elderly people*, discussing the role of reminiscence therapy, and produces a wide range of aids to reminiscence such as quizzes, tapes of nostalgic music, videos, and posters and postcards. Many museums and other organisations organise *reminiscence workshops* for elderly people.

AGE EXCHANGE REMINISCENCE CENTRE

The Age Exchange
The Reminiscence Centre   **Tel: 0181-318 9105**
11 Blackheath Village, London SE3 9LA

This unusual centre has a *memory bank* to which people are invited to contribute. The Age Exchange Reminiscence Project uses music, improvisation, familiar objects and pictures in reminiscence workshops, and The Age Exchange Theatre Company visits homes and performs musical shows based on people's memories.

7

Money

This chapter covers the different sources of income you can store up for old age by saving. Starting with the basic state retirement pension, we also cover other tax allowances, benefits and grants you might be entitled to. Then follows, in a section contributed by Peta Hodge, a look at how you can provide for yourself with a private pension, or make use of other forms of saving like annuities.

Financing old age

Methuselah, grandfather of Noah, was said to be 969 years old when he expired. If he had bought an annuity at the age of 75 for £50,000, in return for a guaranteed income of £10,000 for the rest of his life, he would have bankrupted a small insurance company.

Fortunately for insurance companies and actuaries (who calculate the odds on people surviving beyond a certain age) few people live beyond 100. But if you think you are going to live a long, long time, buying an annuity is just one of many ways of insuring that you don't run out of money to pay the nursing home fees before you too expire.

M&G

Unit Trusts
Life Assurance
Pensions

Three Quays, Tower Hill, London EC3R 6BQ

FINANCING OLD AGE

Before considering pensions, annuities, home income plans and other private sector methods, however, it is worth finding out what you might get from the public sector when you retire, in the form of a state pension or other benefits. State pension support may become means-tested in the next century and some nasty shocks might be avoided by taking action before it is too late.

Basics: the state pension

The *state retirement pension* is paid to anyone who has reached state pensionable age—at present 65 for men and 60 for women—who has met the National Insurance contribution conditions. Your retirement pension is made up of *basic pension* (the 'old age pension') and *additional pension* and is taxable.

The full basic pension in 1995/6 was £58.85 a week for a single person and £94.10 for a married couple. But it is a common mistake to believe that you get that amount regardless of how many years you have worked: the amount of basic pension you get will depend on the number of 'qualifying years' (see box opposite) in your National Insurance contribution record.

To get the minimum basic pension (25 per cent, therefore less than £15 a week for a single person in 1995/6) you must have about nine to ten qualifying years. However:

• You may be able to top up your contributions, by making voluntary Class 3 National Insurance contributions, to get more qualifying years.

• You may be able to get your spouse's NI (National Insurance) record taken into account (even if you are divorced or widowed).

• If you were not able to go out to work because you were looking after someone at home (including children), *home responsibilities protection* (HRP) may be able to reduce the number of qualifying years you need to receive a full basic pension. HRP takes into account the years (from April 1978) when you were not able go out to work.

• Your *additional pension*, known as *state earnings-related pension* (SERPS) depends on your earnings since April 1978 on which you paid Class 1 National Insurance contributions. (National Insurance contributions are divided into classes according to

FINANCING OLD AGE

whether you work full-time, part-time, or are self-employed).

• However, if you are a member of a contracted-out employer's *occupational pension scheme* ('contracting-out' means that the pension scheme takes on the responsibility of providing an occupational pension in place of the additional pension) or if you have a *personal pension* scheme, a deduction will be taken from your (SERPS) additional pension. This is known as the *contracted-out deduction*.

• Widows and widowers may receive the (SERPS) *additional pension* earned by their spouse.

State pension extras

Other additions to the state pension are:

• *Graduated retirement benefit* which depends on the amount of graduated NI contributions you paid between April 1961 and

FINANCING OLD AGE

April 1975.

• *Age addition*, payable to everyone over 80 who satisfies certain residence requirements.

• *Invalidity addition*, which you can get if you received an *invalidity allowance* shortly before you reached pension age.

• You may be able to get *extra pension* for *dependents*.

Worth noting

• Other benefits may reduce your basic pension and vice versa.

• Hospital stays will reduce the amount you receive.

• You can put off receiving your pension for up to five years and earn extra increments.

Useful reading

There are many rulings on pensions covering many differing personal circumstances. For the most accurate picture of current legislation read the DSS booklets: FB6 *Retiring?* and NP46 *A guide to Retirement Pension.* These are available from your local Social Security office and in some post offices and libraries, or from BA Distribution and Storage Centre, Manchester Road, Heywood, Lancashire, OL10 2PZ.

Claiming your state retirement pension

You must claim your *state retirement pension*—it is not sent to you automatically. You should be sent a claim form BR1 about four months before you reach retirement age, so contact your Social Security office if you haven't received one about three months before that time. Any time up to four months before you reach pensionable age, you can get a pension forecast (*form BR19* from your Social Security office). You can claim your pension even if you are still earning—you will no longer have to pay National Insurance contributions. Pensions can be paid directly into your bank or building society account or by a book of orders which are cashed at your post office.

If you are not able to get to the post office, you can nominate an agent (who could be a friend or relative) to collect your pension for you. You can generally have your pension paid anywhere abroad. But beware: if you plan to live abroad in a non-EC country which does not have a reciprocal agreement with the UK

FINANCING OLD AGE

regarding pensions, your pension will not increase when new rates are set in the UK but will remain the same as when you left this country (DSS leaflets NI 106 *Pensioners and widows going abroad* and NI 38 *Social security abroad* will give you further information).

War disablement pensions

If you were disabled as a result of serving in the Armed Forces, or if you were a civilian disabled from a World War II injury, you may be eligible for a *war disablement pension*. War widows and widowers may also be eligible.

• You can phone the War Pension Helpline on 01253-858 858 or write to: The War Pensions Directorate, Norcross, Blackpool, FY5 3TA

...and other state benefits

The regulations governing entitlement to other state benefits can be complicated and confusing.

If you are an oldie yourself or you have ageing relatives who aren't quite on the ball, you can get advice about entitlement from organisations like your local Citizens' Advice Bureau or Help the Aged. Or try the masses of leaflets and booklets, produced by the DSS and the NHS, which explain the different types of benefits available (some of them are listed in brackets in the approriate sections below).

• You can usually find these leaflets at your local social security office or in post offices, libraries or doctor's offices (for those associated with health and illness or disability). If you can't find the leaflets you want you can write to:

For DSS leaflets:

BA Distribution and Storage Centre, Heywood Stores, Manchester Road, Heywood, Lancashire OL10 2PZ

For NHS leaflets:

Health Publications Unit, No. 2 Site, Heywood Stores, Manchester Road, Heywood, Lancashire OL10 2PZ

84

The DSS also runs two telephone advice services. Remember, however, that the person taking your call will not have your personal papers and can only give you general advice.

•**For information about Social Security and National Insurance:**
Freephone Social Security   Tel: 0800-666 555

•**For confidential advice for disabled people and their carers:**
Freephone Benefit Enquiry Line (BEL)   Tel: 0800-882 200

Help on a low income

Income support is the main state benefit for helping people on low incomes. Even a very small amount of income support is worth claiming, because being 'on income support' acts as a sort of means- tested passport to other welfare payments.

Income support

Income support does not depend on National Insurance contributions and can be used to top-up your *state retirement pension*. To claim *income support* you and your partner together must not have more than £8,000 in savings between you and neither of you must be working 16 or more hours a week.

How much you get will depend on you and your partner's income, how much capital you have if your savings are between £3,000 and £8,000, and whether you have any disabilities—among other criteria. You may get help with mortgage interest payments on your home and other housing costs such as service charges. Pensioners get more at age 75 and again at 80. (DSS leaflets IS 1 *Income support* and IS 20 *A guide to income support*). If you are living in a residential care or nursing home you may be able to get help with the fees through *income support* (DSS leaflet IS 50 *Help if you live in a residential care or nursing home*).

Income support usually makes you eligible for other benefits, of which the main ones are housing benefit, council tax benefit, and grants and loans from the Social Fund. People receiving *income support* automatically get help with NHS costs—see opposite.

FINANCING OLD AGE

Housing benefit

Housing benefit is paid by local councils to people on low incomes who need help paying their rent. You do not need to be receiving *income support* to receive *housing benefit* (DSS leaflet RR 1 *Housing benefit—Help with your rent)*.

Council tax benefit

Council tax benefit is also paid by local councils and nearly all the same rules apply as those for receiving housing benefit (DSS leaflet NI 9 *Help with the council tax).*

The Social Fund

The *Social Fund* helps people with expenses which are difficult to pay for out of their regular income. If you are receiving *income support*, you will be eligible for *funeral payments, cold weather payments* to help with heating costs in very cold weather, *community care grants* which help people lead independent lives, and *budgeting loans. Crisis loans* are available to anyone, depending on their income (DSS leaflet SFL 2 *How the social fund can help you*).

Help with NHS costs

Help with NHS costs may be available to you if you fulfil certain eligibility conditions or if you are on a low income— even if you are not receiving *income support*. You can receive free prescriptions (these are available to anyone over retirement age) and dental treatment, free sight tests and money-off vouchers for glasses, free wigs and fabric supports and help with the cost of travelling to hospital for treatment (NHS leaflet AB 11 *Help with NHS costs*).

Help if you are sick or disabled

If you are a woman younger than 65 or a man younger than 70 and not getting your pension, you can claim *sickness benefit* for up to five years after retirement age—that's if you choose not to claim your *state retirement pension* as soon as you reach 60 or 65. This used to be the case for *invalidity benefit* as well. However, as of April 1995 the tax-free invalidity benefit has been replaced by the taxable (certainly for new claimants) *incapacity benefit*. It was expected that following the introduction of the rigorous 'all work' medical test for *incapacity benefit*, more than 500,000 people would lose their right to this benefit over the three years from 1995. The medical test for *invalidity benefit* was meant to satisfy the benefits agency that whoever was making a claim was no longer able to do his or her job. (The 'all work' medical test for *incapacity benefit* is designed to satisfy the benefits agency that whoever is making a claim is no longer able to do *any* work.)

People currently getting *invalidity benefit* (£57.60 a week) were to get instead, depending on the results of a medical test, incapacity benefit (£52.50 a week), which is not earnings-related. However there are exceptions to this rule, and what you decide to claim may affect other benefits you are receiving, so it is as well to get advice from an organisation such as Age Concern or the local Citizen's Advice Bureau to see what decision would be best for you. (DSS leaflet NI 16 *Sickness benefit*, leaflet NI 16A *Invalidity benefit*, and leaflet IB 202 *Incapacity benefit*).

Severe disablement allowance

Severe disablement allowance is tax-free and is usually paid to those who have not made enough National Insurance contributions to claim *sickness benefit* or *invalidity benefit*. It is for people who have been unable to work for at least 28 weeks due to long-term sickness or severe disability (at least 80 per cent disabled). You must be under 65 when you first claim, but once it is claimed it can be paid up to any age. An age-related supplement is paid on top of the standard rate (DSS leaflet NI 252 *Severe disablement allowance*).

Attendance allowance

Attendance allowance is also tax-free and is payable to people over 65 who need a lot of personal care, such as help with eating or going to the lavatory because they are ill or disabled. You do not need to have paid NI contributions. It is not means-tested, nor does it usually count as income when entitlement to income *support* is being calculated.

FINANCING OLD AGE

You or your elderly relative must normally have needed care for six months. If Great-Uncle Archie is terminally ill, however, special rules apply that will enable him to get it sooner. Your elderly relative can go on receiving *attendance allowance* if he goes into a residential care or nursing home that he is paying for privately. If he is receives partial or full support for the fees, however, from a local authority social service department, the *attendance allowance* will be discontinued. (DSS leaflet DS 702 *Attendance allowance* which includes a claim pack).

Disability living allowance

People under 65 should claim *disability living allowance*. (DSS leaflet DS 704 *Disability living allowance*). *Constant attendance allowance* is an extra allowance paid on top of a *war disablement pension* or *industrial injuries disablement benefit*. Your disability must have been assessed at 100 per cent. Constant attendance allowance and attendance allowance cannot be claimed at the same time. (DSS leaflet NI 6 *Industrial injuries disablement benefit*).

Industrial disablement benefit

Industrial disablement benefit may be payable to you if you became ill or disabled as a result of work for an employer after 4 July 1948. It is tax-free and is payable on top of *invalidity benefit, war disablement pension* or *state retirement pension*. You can receive it up to any age. You must be at least 14 per cent disabled, except for some diseases which affect your breathing, and you will be required to have a medical examination. (DSS leaflet NI 6 *Industrial injuries disablement benefit*).

Help if you're a carer

Invalid care allowance (IVC) can be claimed by carers who are looking after someone who is receiving *disability allowance* at the middle or highest rate, *attendance allowance* or *constant attendance allowance*. You must be between 16 and 65 to claim (though you can continue to claim after the age of 65, subject to certain conditions, if you are already receiving IVC) and be spending at least

35 hours per week looking after the invalid. It is not means-tested. Other benefits you receive may cancel out your IVC, but claiming it may be in your interest—for instance if the other benefit is a *widow's benefit*, you can get National Insurance credits by claiming IVC, which could help towards your *State retirement pension* (DSS leaflet FB 31 *Caring for someone?*) For those who care for an elderly relative who is frail but not ill enough for you to qualify for invalid care allowance, it is worth watching the progress of the Carers Bill (see *Chapter 8*).

Saving for yourself

So far this chapter has covered state pensions, benefits and grants for those who find themselves with barely any capital or income when they reach old age. Don't laugh, those of you who have six-figure sums invested in an occupational pension scheme ready for a comfortable retirement. Remember what happened to the Maxwell-controlled company pension schemes? There is another good reason to find out about state financial support in old age when you are still middle-aged—it is often a shock to find out just how little it is, and a shock can force someone to think about their private savings before it gets too late.

Private pensions

The first rule of pension planning is to start early; the second, is that it's never too late to do something. Anyone over the age of 50, who has not already done so, would be well advised to check the value of current private pension arrangements and fund out what can be done to improve them. First, however, there is the option of topping-up your state pension:

Topping up the state pension

You can find out how much state pension you are on target to receive by filling in *form BR19*, available from Department of Social Security (DSS) Benefits Agencies. Women who have had a broken career pattern because of family commitments are likely to be particularly dismayed by the results. However, it may not

FINANCING OLD AGE

be too late to boost your state pension—the DSS will be able to tell you whether it is worth your while to pay some voluntary Class 3 National Insurance contributions in order to do this.

Topping up a company pension

If you are a member of a company pension scheme, you should also find out how much you are on course to receive from this. You may well have been a member of more than one company scheme during your working life. If you have lost track of pensions you have built up with former employers, the Pensions Registry and Tracing Service may be able to help.

•You can contact the Pensions Registry by phoning 0191-225 6437.

Although the Inland Revenue allows you to build up a company pension worth two-thirds of your salary at retirement, few schemes are designed to give you as much as this. Even in a good scheme it can take 40 years of contributions to build up this much. That's why it's a good idea to pay some *additional voluntary contributions* (AVCs) to enhance your company pension.

The tax man allows you to put up to 15 per cent of gross earnings towards your company pension each year. (Although if your earnings are above what is known as the 'earnings cap'—currently set at £78,600 a year—your annual contribution must not exceed 15 per cent of the cap.) Most company pension schemes only require an annual contribution of around 5 per cent of earnings, which means you can pay up to 10 per cent in AVCs.

All employers who run company pension schemes have to offer AVC schemes too. Most of these are run by insurance companies. Alternatively, scheme members can go to an insurance company direct and take out an individual AVC plan, known as a *free-standing additional voluntary contribution* (FSAVC).

There are advantages and disadvantages to both approaches. FSAVCs have recently come in for some flak for being more expensive than group AVCs, but they tend to offer more flexibility and choice; for example, you should be able to take an FSAVC with you if you change jobs and you can choose how the plan is invested. Another advantage of an FSAVC is that your employer doesn't usually have to know you've got one; allowing you to fund quietly for an early retirement if you want to.

Whether contributing to a group AVC or an FSAVC is best for you will depend on your personal circumstances—there's nothing to stop you contributing to both types of plan so long as you stick to the 15 per cent overall contribution limit. Of course, you don't have to invest in an AVC plan at all—you can top up your pension using an ordinary investment or savings plan. One of the attractions of AVCs, however, is that—as with other types of pension plan—you get full tax relief on all contributions.

Topping up a personal pension

If you contribute to a *personal pension* rather than a *company pension* scheme, you may also want to consider increasing your contributions. As a rough rule of thumb, you need to have around £100,000 in the pot to secure an annual pension of £10,000.

The amount you are allowed to contribute to a personal pension increases with age. If you are between age 46 and 50 your contributions are limited to 25 per cent of your earnings up to the earnings cap (see above). Between 51 and 55 the limit is 30 per cent, between 56 and 60 the limit is 35 per cent and between 61 and 74 you can contribute up to 40 per cent. (If you have one of the old-style personal pensions (known as *S226's* or *retirement annuity contracts*) which was set up before 1988, the contributions limits are lower—but you can still contribute up to the new limits by taking out a new personal pension alongside.)

The personal pension is unique in also allowing you to 'mop up' unused contribution limits (and tax relief) from previous years. The mechanisms for doing this are known as 'carry forward' and 'carry back'—anyone wanting to make use of them should seek advice from an accountant or financial adviser.

Personal pensions: consolidating gains

With a personal pension, the amount you contribute is only half the story—the pension you get out at the end will also depend on how your investments perform. By the time you reach the age of 50, your personal pension will already have enjoyed significant investment growth. As you approach retirement, it is important that you consolidate these gains.

This means gradually switching out of equities (company shares, where the value of investments can fall as well as rise) and into investments such as fixed-interest deposits and cash where capital is secure. The rate at which individuals switch will depend to some extent on their temperament—some of us are more prepared to take risks than others. But by the time they are within two years of retirement, most people will want to have off-loaded their equity exposure. They will want to be sure that if the stock market crashes a year before they retire, they are not going to see their pension cut in half.

Timing the move out of equities can be tricky. Clearly the aim is to sell equities when they are relatively expensive and buy capital-secure investments when they are relatively cheap. Anyone who is not experienced in managing investments should seek professional financial advice on this. Some personal pension plans include an automatic switching facility so that you don't have to make these difficult decisions yourself.

Is it too late to start?

It is true that the earlier you start saving for your pension, the better the pension you will end up with. But if you have reached the age of 50 and still haven't started it's still not too late to do something.

Anyone offered the chance to join a *company pension* scheme in the last few years before retirement would usually be advised to take it—apart from anything else, the employer usually makes a sizeable contribution, so turning down the chance to join would be a bit like volunteering for a pay cut. Having joined a company pension scheme, it would usually make sense for the individual to put as much as he or she could afford into AVCs.

Personal pension charges

For those who don't have the opportunity to join a company pension scheme, a *personal pension* scheme may be the answer. However, charges on some of these personal pension plans can be on the hefty side and the nearer you are to retirement, the less time you have to cover the charges through investment performance. It should also be said that charges tend to hit small contributions particularly hard. So it's important to shop around and find a personal pension that gives a good deal on charges. Having said all that, tax relief available on contributions will usually compensate for the most punitive of charging structures—even as a basic tax rate payer, for every £750 you contribute to a pension, the Inland Revenue chips in another £250.

Are there any alternatives?

Pension plans do have their drawbacks. One of the problems is that you can't take any money out until you are ready to start drawing your pension. Another problem is that pensions are designed to provide income—you can only take a relatively small proportion of your benefits as a lump sum (25 per cent in the case of *personal pensions*). On the other hand, the big attraction of pensions, of course, is the tax relief.

Personal equity plans

Personal equity plans (PEPs) come close to pensions on this. Instead of getting tax relief on contributions, you get it on the proceeds. As with pensions, high-rate taxpayers have the most to gain. One of the problems of using a PEP as a pension, however, is that you're buying out-and-out stock exchange exposure. Another is that you can only invest £6,000 in a PEP each year (plus £3,000 in a 'single company' PEP). As with personal pensions and FSAVCs, PEP charges can be on the high side. Although you can get at money invested in PEPs at any time, as with other types of equity investment, you are only likely to do well if you leave your money where it is for several years.

Tessas

Tax exempt special savings plans (TESSAs) also offer considerable tax savings, but you have to leave your money tied up for five years in order to get them and over the five-year period you may only invest a total of £9,000. There is probably a place for a PEP and a TESSA in the financial planning of most taxpayers. But

FINANCING OLD AGE

most experts would suggest that these and other types of investment are used as well as, not instead of, a proper pension scheme.

Buying an annuity

Company pensions tend to be paid directly out of the company pension scheme. But in the past, if you saved for retirement with a *personal pension*, you were not allowed to take your pension income directly from the personal pension plan. Instead, you had to use the bulk of the fund you had built up to 'buy' an annuity —an annual income for life—from an insurance company.

The level annuity

There are various different types of annuity. A *level annuity* pays you exactly the same fixed level of pension from the day you retire to the day you die. The attraction of this type of annuity is that it gives you a good deal in the first few years of retirement. The problem with a level annuity is that you get no protection against inflation. Bearing in mind that you may be receiving this pension for more than 20 years, the impact of rising prices should not be ignored, especially when you consider that, even with just 1 per cent inflation, £1,000 invested today would be worth £820 in 20 years' time.

Escalating and unit-linked annuities

That's why most people would be advised to buy an *escalating annuity*. There are various types available: some increase by a fixed amount each year, typically 3 per cent or 5 per cent; and some increase in line with the Retail Prices Index (RPI).

There is a price to pay for inflation proofing, however. The insurance company that provides the pension has to hold back money to pay for future pension increases, so you will get a much smaller pension in the early years than with a level pension. For those prepared to take a bit of a risk, a few insurance companies offer investment-linked arrangements known as *with-profits annuities* and *unit-linked annuities*, where the pension received increases (or falls) in line with the underlying investments.

Annuity with a pension?

Another point you need to consider when buying an annuity is whether you want to provide your spouse with a pension after your death. Again, this can be a valuable benefit but will mean reducing your own pension. Likewise, for a further reduction in your pension, you can buy a guarantee that your pension will be paid for a specified period—typically five or ten years—even if you die before that period is up.

It is important to remember that you don't have to buy your annuity from the company that runs your personal pension. You have the option to shop around and it's a good idea to take it—there can be as much as 30 per cent difference between the top and bottom rates available at any time. A word of warning, however: if you have an old-style pre-1988 personal pension, buying an annuity on the open market could reduce the amount of tax free cash you may take from your pension plan—so it's a good idea to get financial advice before taking the plunge.

Flexible annuities

Annuity rates go up and down with interest rates, so it's a bit of a lottery whether or not you get good value for money. This is one reason why the government has recently allowed the introduction of *flexible annuities*. These controversial products allow you to delay annuity purchase. Instead, you can take a certain amount of income directly out of the pension plan each year (as long as it is not more than 100 per cent and not less that 35 per cent of what you would have got from a conventional annuity.) In the meantime, the rest of your pension plan stays invested, giving the potential for further investment growth. You must at some time buy a conventional annuity, but you can delay until your 75th birthday if you want to.

The *flexible annuity* may be particularly attractive to those who want the flexibility to vary the amount of pension they take each year, as well as those who want to put off buying an annuity until rates improve. There are potential risks involved with this type of annuity, however. For example, the value of the fund that remains invested could fall instead of rise and annuity rates could get worse rather than better.

What about the tax-free cash?

Income tax is paid on pension income, but company pension schemes and personal pensions allow you to forgo some of your pension and take some of the benefits you have built up as a tax free cash lump sum. (As mentioned above, you don't get tax free cash from AVCs).

Because of the tax relief, it's nearly always advisable to take the cash—even if your main need is for income rather than capital; you can always use the cash to buy a special kind of annuity, known as a *purchased life annuity*—this can work out considerably more tax efficient than using the whole pension fund to buy a conventional annuity.

Investment at retirement

Many people at or near retirement find, often for the first time in their lives, that they may have serious amounts of money to invest. In many cases, as well as a tax-free lump sum from a pension, there is cash from maturing insurance policies. For those who decide that retirement is the time to move somewhere smaller, there may even be the proceeds from the sale of the family home.

Capital versus income

The important thing is to be clear about your investment aims. With luck, your various pension arrangements will provide enough income to meet your day-to-day living expenses, so your main concern is likely to be capital growth. You are no longer working, so the money you have now has to last for the rest of your life—another 30 years or more, perhaps. You therefore have a tricky balancing act to perform. If you attempt to maximise capital growth, for example by investing in equities, you risk depleting your capital if stock markets fall. On the other hand, if you go all-out for capital protection, for example by putting your cash in a building society account, over time the value of your capital is likely to be eaten away by inflation. There is no one right answer to the problems of investing after retirement. Much will depend on personal circumstances and personal attitude to risk. If you are a taxpayer, you should almost certainly take out a TESSA if you haven't already got one.

Steady interest

Having said that, in most cases it makes sense to have a well-funded savings account, which will provide you with easy access to cash in an emergency. Reports abound, however, of older people who keep £10,000 or more in a current account, earning nothing, because 'when something happens to me I'll need to get the money out quickly.' If you find Great-Aunt Annie's bank manager is letting this situation go unremarked, you can justifiably be angry about it. Few older people need to have more than £1,000 in a current account. In an emergency funds can be easily transferred at, say, 14 days notice, from a high-interest deposit account.

Fixed-interest investments have the attraction of guaranteeing to pay the investor a specified capital sum at a set date in the future. They also provide a fixed level of income each year. Gilts are the best known fixed-interest investment and provide the extra comfort factor of being backed by the government. If you don't want to buy gilts direct, you could buy into a managed gilt fund. These are unit trusts where investors' money is pooled and an expert fund manager invests in gilts on their behalf. Both types if investment offer capital security and steady, unspectacular growth.

Or adventurous equities?

For those who have the resources and temperament to take the risk, equity investment offers the potential for the best long-term returns. PEPs may be suitable for some people; others may think that unit or investment trusts are the best way for them to invest in the stock market. Insurance company investment bonds also

FINANCING OLD AGE

invest mainly in equities are for long term investors—if you can't afford to tie your money up for three years of more, think again. And remember, the value of equity investments can fall as well as rise.

This guidebook can only touch on the investment options available. It's important that, whatever your circumstances and attitude to risk, you get professional financial advice on the solutions to meet your meeds. Remember too that your needs will change as you get older.

In your 50s or 60s, your priority is likely to be capital growth. But by the time you're 70, you may be more interested in income. You may even consider raise money on your home through a *home income plan*, for example. These controversial schemes do have considerable drawbacks, however, and should only be entered into after careful thought and proper financial advice.

Care fee planning

Increased life expectancy means that more elderly people will be living in nursing or residential care homes. Many older people will see their life savings or the proceeds from their former homes disappear as the return on their money falls short of the cost of care and accommodation, and in some cases the money will run out before the need for care ceases.

It is important to seek specialist financial advice when planning to cover care fees, as most normal financial advisers are not fully aware of the financial and legal complexities of the care system. The Nursing Home Fees Agency, for example, advises clients to split their joint accounts into two single accounts as soon as the need for care arises.

As mentioned in Chapter 10, the DSS and the local authority take into account joint savings with a spouse left at home when assessing a prospective resident's entitlement to financial help with care home fees. Until these joint savings fall to £16,000 (that is, the £8,000 eligibility limit for each person) no financial help will be available. By dividing the joint account into two separate accounts a substantial saving can be made and state assistance can be obtained earlier.

FINANCING OLD AGE

• *Information* Further advice or a free fact pack on purchasing care can be obtained from: The Nursing Home Fees Agency, FREEPOST, Old Bank House, 95 London Road, Headington, Oxford, 0X3 9AE.

Long-term care insurance

Long-term care insurance is a fairly new concept in the UK and only a few companies offer such contracts. Long-term care insurance policies can be used to provide care in your own home or in a residential or nursing home. Some companies will also allow money to be spent on adapting your home for disability. The two basic types of long term care insurance are:

• *Regular premium contracts:* These set a monthly premium depending on the age and health of the insured and the level of fees to be covered.

• *Single premium contracts:* These take the form of a lump sum premium. As with regular premium contracts the cost will depend on your circumstances, and the healthier you are and the earlier you take a policy, the lower the premiums.

There are a few concerns that should be looked at before making any decision:

• Will the premiums increase and can you afford them in retirement?

• Do you want to cover home care or nursing care only?

• Can you assume that a spouse will be a carer or should you cover both lives?

• Has the policy paid up value or death benefit and what happens if you stop paying the premiums?

• What activities of daily living (ADLs) need to be impaired and for how long before claims are paid? Common ADL tests are:

• Are you mobile, able to get around from room to room, not necessarily including stairs?

• Can you dress yourself unaided?

• Can you feed yourself unaided?

• Can you walk properly unaided?

• Can you use the lavatory unaided?

• Can you move on your own from a bed to an upright chair?

FINANCING OLD AGE

Benefits or half-benefits may be paid when failing two to three activities of daily living described above, depending on the insurance company and the cover taken. Before considering such a policy, find out what period the benefits would be paid for, and if a tax advantage can be gained by making benefits payable direct to a nursing home. You also need to make sure that the family or solicitor is aware of the existence of such a policy in case you are too unwell to make a claim yourself.

Financial advice

If you are at or near retirement, you have some particularly tough financial decisions to make. Few people feel able to make these decisions alone. If you don't already have an accountant or financial adviser to help you, you should find one. IFA Promotions, a commercial company, keeps a list of 4,000 firms offering independent financial advice. It will also send you some useful information about how to find independent financial advice.

• *Information* You can get a list of three independent advisers in your area by phoning the IFA (Tel: 0171-831 4027). The Money Management Council (Tel: 01992 503 448) also produces a leaflet entitled *Where can I get financial advice?* For advice about pensions you can phone the Department of Employment's Occupational Pension Advice Line (Tel: 0171-233 8080).

Power of attorney

Great-Aunt Annie can no longer remember her *tour de force* as
Gertrude confronting Hamlet. In fact, she has mistaken her son
Fred for Hamlet on his latest visit and is now unable to tell the
difference between a dividend slip and a parking ticket. Time for
someone to think about an EPA?

Enduring Power of Attorney (EPA) authorises another person to
manage the financial affairs of someone who, due to an accident,
illness or advancing years, is no longer able to do so. An attorney
can pay bills, check bank statements, prepare tax returns, apply
for benefit payments, collect your income, deal with your house,
insure it, repair it, or arrange for it to be sold. However an attorney cannot take decisions that have nothing to do with money.
He or she cannot, for example, make a Will for you.

An EPA is a simple document that can be completed quickly
and inexpensively by a solicitor. Although an EPA can be used
as soon as it has been signed, it is usual to sign an EPA in case
you fall ill or have an accident, and the document is kept safe in
the same way as a Will.

You are free to choose anyone you like to act as your attorney,
but it should be someone who you can trust and who will act in
your best interests and deal with your affairs promptly. The
Nursing Home Fees Agency suggests that, for additional peace
of mind, it is useful to have two attorneys, and that one of them
is a solicitor .

Making a will

Although everyone tries to make some sort of provision for retirement, fewer people make any arrangements for their death. Perhaps not wishing to tempt fate, seven out of every ten people never make a will. As a result the valued possessions of someone who dies intestate, without making a will, may not be distributed as the owner would have liked. Intestacy can also leave complicated work to be done by relatives who have to sort out the legal mess afterwards. • Advice: get your solicitor to help you to make a tax-efficient will, keep it fair and simple and tell the family it is not likely to be altered except in an emergency.

Glossary of legal terms

Most of the following terms have quite simple meanings, but you may get to know them until after someone has died.

Administrators

People who manage and distribute your estate if you do not make a will.

Beneficiary

Anyone who benefits from your will.

Codicil

An additional document to alter an existing will. This must be signed and witnessed in the same legal manner as your will, and both documents should be kept together. Codicils are for minor alterations to a will: if you want to make big changes you should draw up a completely new document. Do not try to change a will by crossing parts out, adding words in or attaching anything to it, as you could invalidate the will.

Crown

The Treasury. This is where your money (your estate) goes if you have no next of kin and did not make a will.

Estate

The total of what you leave, including any money, property and possessions.

Executors

People you appoint to ensure the instructions in your will are carried out. It's standard practice to name two executors, a *first executor* (usually a spouse) and a younger *second executor* (son or daughter). Executors cannot be forced to handle your estate personally, and they can take professional help on any or all aspects dealing with the estate.

Inheritance tax

Taxes due on your death (previously known as *death duties* or *capital transfer tax*). Your estate may be liable to inheritance tax. The whole or any part of your estate left to your husband or wife is exempt from tax. All gifts to charity are currently tax free.

Intestacy

Dying without making a valid will.

Legacy

There are three types of legacy. A *specific legacy* is a single item given in a will, like a gold watch. A *pecuniary legacy* is a sum of money. And a *residuary legacy* is the residue or share of an estate left in a will.

Probate

Probate often means the issuing of a legal document to one or more people authorising them to deal with the dead person's estate, once it has been established whether the will is valid and who are the will's administrators or executors.

Residue

What is left of your estate after payment of debts, funeral expenses, taxes and legacies.

Testator

The person making the will.

Witness

Two people over the age of 18 are required to witness your will. Neither of the witnesses, nor their partners, may benefit from your will.

FINANCING OLD AGE

What to do

Carefully note and value, at today's prices, everything you own (such as property, personal possessions, insurance policies, building society, bank and National Savings accounts, stocks and shares) less anything you owe (mortgages, hire purchase agreements, bank overdrafts or other debts). This will give you a pretty good idea of your estate's present value. It is worth bearing in mind that your funeral expenses will be met by your estate, so set aside some money to cover these. You should then clearly list each item of personal property you want to mention in your will and the person you want to leave it to. You should also write down the full names and addresses of the people and institutions you want to name as beneficiaries, and the details of the people or organisations who have agreed to act as executors.

Do-it-yourself or not?

Although you can draw up a do-it-yourself Will necessary forms that are available in most newsagents, it is advisable to go to a solicitor to make sure that your wishes are carried out correctly after your death. A DIY Will can save you money, but a Will drawn up by a solicitor can cover every eventuality and ensure that your Will is legally proven. The money saved on a home - made document will not be enough to cover the legal costs of sorting out your estate if you make one incorrectly.

The cost of general work like drawing up a Will depends on each solicitor's hourly rate, usually between £50 and £70 an hour, and an additional profit mark-up which is usually 50 per cent. The Law Society publishes a leaflet that explains how the Society assesses solicitors' charges for general work. The example used in the leaflet has a solicitor giving tax planning advice to a husband and wife and preparing a new Will for both of them. The solicitor takes four hours to complete the work and his hourly expense rate is £70, so the cost for his time is £280. Once the 50 per cent mark-up of £140 has been added, the total cost comes to £420. However, the leaflet ends with the words: "Please note that the Society cannot take into account the fact that other solicitors may have been prepared to charge less for carrying out the work."

8

Community care and the social services

In Chapter 2: The Framework, we outlined changing government policies and the way national and local authorities divide responsibility for the welfare of older people. As a result of the NHS and Community Care Act, local authority social services now play the main role in this framework. It is important to know how social service departments work and how they co-ordinate with other organisations. Your social service care manager could be a key figure.

The Community Care Act

There has been turmoil in local authority social services since the 1990 *NHS and Community Care Act* took full effect in April 1993. If you are now confused about who deals with services for the old, frail, mentally ill or disabled, you are not alone.

COMMUNITY CARE

The government's community care strategy has brought about radical change in the way older people are looked after. The idea is that no-one should be kept in an institution (for example, a long-stay bed in a hospital geriatric ward) any longer than necessary, and that everything possible should be done to help them stay in their own homes instead, with support services from local social service departments and health authorities.

For the majority of people who would like to spend a dignified old age in their own homes, but who need some help to enable them to do so, this should be excellent news. Unfortunately, however, many people with savings now find they have to pay for their own 'domiciliary care' where before they would have been looked after, free, in hospital.

Although the Act makes local authorities responsible for looking after elderly people (among others who cannot look after themselves), the only statutory duty imposed on them is to assess old people's needs. However, once the assessment has

UNDERWHELMED

"Whatever their uncertainties and ambivalence about charging for services, carers are not in doubt about the impact of the comunity care changes. Nearly 80% of all the carers in this survey said that the changes had made no difference to them, and 8% thought that services had got worse."

'Community Care: Just a Fairy Tale', survey for Carers National Association by Norman Warner, March 1994

COMMUNITY CARE

WHO PAYS FOR COUNCIL SERVICES?

The starting point is a set of figures from the government. The government thinks that services provided by Oxfordshire County Council should cost £312 million. The government also sets an expenditure cap for Oxfordshire County Council at £316 million. The Council has decided to spend at this limit in 1995/6. Who pays? On average it works out like this:

	TOTAL	£ per head
Council tax	£95m	£161
Government grant	£115m	£196
Business rates*	£106m	£182
	£316m	£182

*Business rates are set by the government
Oxfordshire County Council 1995/96

been made the local authority must provide the necessary services. As far as practical help is concerned, it is then up to individual councils to decide how much to spend and who to help according to the priorities set by these assessments of need, and this can mean providing excellent support services or virtually none. Only when each local resident get down to his or her last £8,000 (excluding the family home) are they entitled to free support in their own homes, a residential care home or a nursing home. How well infirm relatives are looked after, therefore, depends on which local authority area they live in: some councils provide first-class support services, others virtually none.

Those who have enough money saved to tide them through old age may never come into contact with social workers except after a stay in hospital: they will hire their own home help and choose their own nursing homes if they need to move. With cases of 'rationed' hospital care hitting the headlines, however, many are worried about their future. If you want to make sure Great Aunt Annie is given all the help she can get, it can be useful to know what goes on in the social services department of a local authority. This department may be crucial in the future, however comfortable she is now. And as more information about the work of local authorities is released (for example in Audit Commission reports) it will become easier for you to monitor her local council's performance in looking after elderly people.

107

COMMUNITY CARE

Local authorities

Like almost everything else in Britain, local authorities are being restructured, and in 1995 many were due to be converted into 'unitary' authorities. The money they spend on helping your great-aunt, however, will still be yours (as a taxpayer, through the goverment grant) or hers (through the council tax on her house), so you both have a right to see that it is well spent.

How community care works

Local councils used to provide a wide range of services like day care centres and meals on wheels by developing property themselves and employing their own staff to work in them. Recently, because they have had to spend 85 per cent of their social service funds (special transitional grant) in the private sector, they act more as agents, paying independent businesses and voluntary organisations to provide the care services local people need.

Only a minority of older people receive help with their daily needs from local social services. Most are cared for by husbands, wives and families, often without any respite—the chance to take a break by having someone else take over their responsibilities.

PERCENTAGE OF PEOPLE OVER 75 HELPED TO LIVE AT HOME
Top ten councils

LONDON	METROPOLITAN	COUNTY
City of London	Sunderland	Gwynedd
Islington	Calderdale	Derbysgure
Hackney	Wakefield	Mid-Glamorgan
Tower Hamlets	Leeds	Staffordshire
Newham	South Tyneside	Gwent
Barking & Dag.	Barnsley	Humberside
Hammersmith & Ful.	Sandwell	Cleveland
Camden	Salford	Northumberland
Waltham Forest	Gateshead	Clwyd
Merton	Manchester	Dyfed
London average 15%	Met. average 16%	County average 11%

Source: Audit Commission Local Authority Performance Indicators 1995

HOW OLD IS ELDERLY?

It depends who you are talking to. The Audit Commission, which publishes performance indicators on local authorities, has defined 'elderly' as 'over 75' for its league tables. Most local authorities, however, count you in for services once you are old enough to get a state pension. That means 60 for women and 65 for men (until April 2010, when the retirement age for women starts to rise to 65). But being an OAP does not guarantee you a service. You don't get meals-on-wheels delivered just because you can't be bothered to cook—you have to be assessed to see if you really need them.

More than six million people look after a dependent spouse, relative or friend, according to the Carers National Association. Yet increasing life expectancy and the reduction in NHS long-stay beds means that more help than ever is needed for older people at home.

This may sound gloomy, but it does not mean that services will not be provided. What it does mean is that access to community care will depend on when you apply, whether or not your GP is

---

NIGHTS OF RESPITE CARE PER 1,000 ADULTS
Top ten councils

LONDON	METROPOLITAN	COUNTY
Brent	Bradford	Lancashire
Barking & Dag.	Rochdale	Cornwall
Harrow	Oldham	Cumbria
Bexley	Tameside	Staffordshire
Waltham Forest	Sefton	Lincolnshire
Lewisham	Sheffield	Kent
Enfield	Salford	Oxfordshire
Merton	Coventry	North Yorkshire
Haringey	Sunderland	West Glamorgan
Sutton	Kirklees	Suffolk
London average 52 nights	Met. average 66 nights	County average 66 nights

Source: Audit Commission Local Authority Performance Indicators 1995 Vol 1

COMMUNITY CARE

HOW MUCH FOR SOCIAL SERVICES?

Here is a clear explanation from Oxfordshire County Council (OCC), which needed to raise £95 million from council tax-payers in Oxfordshire in 1995/6: If you own a house worth £52,001-£68,000 (council tax band C), you pay £1.09 a day in council tax. Of that, 22p a day goes to social services. And OCC social services says that it:

- works with 22,245 people each day;
- receives 100 new referrals each day;
- provides 800,000 hours of home care each year involving 1,000,000 visits;
- supports 1,000 residential places for elderly people in 22 county homes and a further 500 in nursing and independent homes.
- undertakes 1,700 child protection investigations each year;
- looks after 450 children each day in foster placements and in children's homes.

---

on your side, how badly you need help, and whether there are local advocates willing and able to help you get the services you need. Most councils will provide a service assessment for people who need some help in the home to enable them to continue living independent lives. The amount of service given will depend as much on the council's available resources—both personnel and finance—as on the individual's needs.

HOME HELP

Are you a bit wobbly? What Camden Council does for frail pensioners (subject to an assessment) is typical of many other local social service departments. It will send a visiting home help to:

- do housework, including ironing;
- do your shopping for you, including collecting your pension;
- if you are extremely weak, get you out of bed in the morning and help to give you a wash or bath; and
- make breakfast for you in your own home.

If you are on benefit, the service costs £2 a week; if not £3.60 a week. However if you are receiving care services worth £220 a week or more you are financially assessed and may have to contribute £40-£60 a week. For anyone else, there is a standing charge of £3 a week which covers all the services provided.

COMMUNITY CARE

The assessment

Comprehensive community care assessments are carried out when an individual has much greater need for help. This assessment, usually carried out by a social or health worker, a care manager or an occupational therapist, will look at a person's need for practical help in the home, which may include help with washing and dressing from round-the-clock care attendants. The result will be either the drawing up of a care plan or package to provide the services needed to maintain the person in his or her own home, or a decision that the person needs to go into a residential care home or nursing home (*see Chapter 10: Homes*). In both cases, the care plan or the decision about going into a home should be made in consultation with the elderly person and whoever is caring for him or her.

Home help

The most common problem for people who suffer simply from old age is lack of strength. Without this, easy daily tasks like getting up, climbing stairs and walking become a great strain. So what most social service (domiciliary care or home care) departments do is draw up a care plan, which is rather like a timetable or 'menu' of services covering the tasks which need strength .

The care plan

The care plan for a normal week, for example, might include sending out a care worker to an elderly person's home for two hours three times a week to carry out the sort of jobs that a son, daughter or neighbour might otherwise do—like shopping, collecting a pension cheque, washing and ironing. Added to this might be a twice weekly visit from, say, a care worker who will help to get Granny out of bed and washed or bathed. Then there will be a meals-on-wheels delivery every weekday, when a charity worker brings in a hot meal. Local authorities are now beginning to charge for some of these services, except for people who are on income support or down to a means-tested level of £3,000 to £8,000 of savings (the level depends on the service provided).

111

COMMUNITY CARE

THE CARE NETWORK: MEDICAL

While an elderly patient is ill or convalescing at home, or has a condition that needs medical supervision, the GP and medical staff who operate under the local health authority take responsibility. These are:

• The GP (general practitioner) in cases of illness and patients discharged from hospital.

• The district nurse. A qualified RGN that provides nursing care at home. Usually you are referred to a district nurse by your GP.

• The health visitor. A trained nurse that gives help and advice on health issues and personal welfare in the home. You do not have to be referred to a health visitor.

• The occupational therapist gives help and information on coping with daily tasks.

THE CARE NETWORK: SOCIAL SERVICES

•The medical team will liaise with the social services team during this period. When the person concerned is no longer ill, but simply frail, the social services team will take over. These are:

• The co-ordinator of all the social services you are likely to need for an elderly relative is the social worker in the social services department who has been assigned to the case.

THE CARERS: DEFINITIONS

• CARED-FOR The cared-for is the old and frail person who should be helped by all the people listed below.

• CARER The carer is the person who looks after a dependent who is unable to look after himself or herself.

• CARE WORKER A paid outsider who comes in to give practical help with household tasks or carry out other tasks that do not need nursing qualifications.

• CARER SUPPORT WORKER The person, usually in a social services department, who supports carers (see box later in this chapter).

Getting good service

How do you know if you are getting good enough service? Once the care assessment and the care plan (you are entitled to a written copy) have been completed, you can compare the level of care received with the level of care promised. The qualifications

GRIPES

Nursing home proprietors complain about the loss of business resulting from the Community Care Act. Abuses they and others point out are:

• Inefficiency of social services in some local authorities and an obsession with unnecessary management procedures and paperwork.

• Lack of financial guidelines on services provided. For example, a willingness to fund £600 a week of home help and other services when an elderly person would be quite happy to go into a nursing home at half the cost.

• The unfair advantage of local authorities in recommending their own care homes. Many of these, according to independent nursing home owners, have now been converted into trusts and social service workers still recommend them to older people without relatives who are too confused to choose for themselves.

and experience, not to mention social skills and punctuality, of the social or voluntary workers involved in the care plan may vary considerably. Reported cases of incompetence include, for example, a very old pensioner being left alone and unable to move from his chair for three days because a care worker did not turn up. If you, a relative, have a copy of the care plan, you should know exactly who is responsible for each service, and when.

Should the realities of community care not live up to expectations, a complaint can be made to the complaints officer of your local authority's social services department. If the matter cannot be resolved informally the complaint should be put in writing. Complaints can be made on behalf of somebody else. The local Community Health Council has experience in handling complaints. CHC staff can offer advice and help you draw up a written complaint.

OVERHEARD

"The meals on wheels are disgusting. It's usually carrots and mashed potato in a pool of glue... Mustn't grumble."

COMMUNITY CARE

Country carers

Patrick Leavey does not wear a grey suit. Corduroys and a sweater are his kit for a day's disciplined work as the manager of the Henley-on-Thames social services team, which serves a population of around 20,000 people, stretching out from the town to surrounding villages.The Henley social service department is in turn one of Oxfordshire County Council's 14 local social service offices.

Working in the Henley team are eight care managers who organise services (like visiting meals on wheels) supplied by half-a-dozen care agencies to families needing help. The care manager also acts as the co-ordinator for a particular case, and at the Henley office each one has a workload of 60-100 cases. "Some are straightforward," explains Leavey. "Others are very complicated, needing up to six visits a day. "A local authority has to provide services defined according to need for care, not by age—we expect to provide service for all high-priority cases, and we would like to provide services for the medium and lower priority ones."

Henley's care managers in turn work with home care assistants, the people who actually help old people face-to-face. Some 50 of these, part-time and full-time, are employed directly or through the outside agencies or charities to which it subcontracts tasks.

"We liaise with other offices in Oxfordshire,"says Leavey. "If it's practical for someone to go to a day centre in another district, we will try to arrange it... Because the care manager is an agent for services a sum of money can then be agreed for spending on, say, nursing home fees. So, depending on the agreed charge band, you could ask the council to buy a bed for your elderly parent in a nursing home nearer you."

Financial support for carers

The Carers Act (see box below) is expected to make it easier for people to stay in their own homes longer if they have a reasonably fit relative or friend to care for them. Supporters of this legislation have been campaigning for carers to be given more financial support in recognition of the duties they undertake.

114

Carers would then be able to support themselves better, afford to take an occasional break, receive more respite breaks for their dependents or pay for extra help. This in turn should mean that people will not need to be moved permanently into nursing homes earlier than necessary.

Respite care

Respite care means giving a carer a break (for example, if you are half an elderly couple, from having to get up repeatedly in the night, every night of the year, to help your wife get to the bathroom). Respite care can mean bringing help into the home for a period to give you a complete rest (for example, by providing a night-sitting care worker for a few nights) or taking the problem out of your home for a few days a week to give you a rest.

Charities or local authorities that provide the service usually do so by admitting the cared-for person into a nursing home for a few days, because providing nightsitting services is expensive. Alternatively, the respite can be given by sending someone out to look after the cared-for and giving the exhausted carer a few days in a rest home instead.

Usually the first way a social service department helps to relieve the stress of caring for an elderly relative is to arrange to have him or her taken into a day care centre, say, two or three days a week.

THE CARERS (Recognition and Services) BILL

A Carers Bill that by April 1995 had passed its second reading in the House of Lords was expected to become law later in the year. It is non-party political legislation that will give greater recognition and financial support for carers, those people who look after dependent relatives or friends. .The Act is expected to recognise that carers (defined as people who spend a certain minimum number of hours a week looking after the personal care of a dependent—bathing, feeding and lifting for example). Under the Act it is also likely that from April 1996 social service departments will have a statutory duty to assess the needs of carers as well as the people they care for, to see if carers can also be provided with services such as respite.

COMMUNITY CARE

The day care centre

This subject comes up when the daily rota of kind neighbours and home helps is no longer enough. Great-Aunt Annie is fitter than Great-Uncle Archie but can no longer cope. They are both now 85. He is constantly tripping over his walking stick and she can't pick him up; she is losing temper and weight with equal speed. Something more must be done. Their niece (still living 100 miles away) calls the social service care manager who is handling the case and asks about day care centres.

CARING FOR THE CARER

"If a case is serious, like looking after someone with Alzheimer's disease, the carer can have planned respite. We could take the person who is unable to look after himself into a home, say, for one week in every five." Margaret Lewis, primary care manager in Greenwich, which has a Carers Centre.

These centres can range from small places where quite healhty OAPs can meet for lunch to ones that are equipped to deal with, say, the near-blind and incontinent. Just as importantly, they vary according to the people who inhabit them. If Archie is a stiff-upper-lip military man, he may not want to be left with a dozen ladies who knit. And if he is no more than eccentric and forgetful, allowing him to be taken to a centre for the mentally ill would be cruel.

Although a local authority will normally take an elderly person to the nearest day care centre they should give him and his family some choice. If you don't think the social worker understands your ageing relative well enough to make the right choice, the best thing you can do is arrange a tour of day centres to see for yourself, and lobby on his behalf. When admission days have been arranged, transport to and from the day centre will usually be provided by a local authority minibus. Sometimes taxis are also used to take non-urgent clients to and from their home to the day centre, clinic or hospital.

Going to a day care centre is usually a point when tension arises between an elderly couple. He does not want to be 'carted away'. She cannot take any more stress. The situation has to be resolved, or it will get worse. Great-Uncle may have to be told that if he doesn't give Great-Aunt a break, she will collapse and die. The solution can be to ask for more respite care, by taking him into a care home for a week, or a 'GP bed' in a hospital, although GP beds are still relatively rare.

Going into a home

The next stage after day care centre sessions and other respite breaks may be an even more difficult decision about going into a

COMMUNITY CARE

home, particularly if it looks like a trip up a one-way street. If you suspect that an assessment will lead to a decision that a residential care or nursing home (*see Chapter 10*) is the best answer, it is advisable to apply for accommodation through a social worker, even if you expect to meet the full cost of the fees. This will ensure that your local council will take some responsibility for the fees at a later stage when it may no longer be possible to meet them. This is beginning to happen because of the complicated financial rules that apply.

The financial rules

Where older people have capital assets of less than £8,000, a local authority may help with the cost of care home or nursing home fees. If they own their own house or flat, its value can count towards the £8,000 limit. This has led to family homes being sold to pay for nursing home fees, and speculation that in future people will have to take out insurance against the cost of future home fees instead of being able to rely on state funding. *(See Chapters 7 & 10.)*

Access to community care services is through a social worker, but many people will turn for help first to their GP. This is also a useful approach because the GP will refer the case to the local social service department, and may provide medical evidence to back up a claim for help at home or a residential place.

Although it is not always possible to plan, it is important to ask for a social services assessment at the right time. If it is more than half way through a financial year, a request may be refused because the community care budget has been spent. But once a council accepts responsibility for providing a service, it is a lifetime commitment. The service must continue for as long as it is needed.

People who apply for a service may be offered a limited amount of help or be asked to reapply in six months time. If you feel the need is more urgent, it is important to get as many people with influence on your side as possible, such as your GP, local councillors, local pressure groups (like Age Concern, *see Chapter 5*) and your MP.

These people may also help to get the health services you need. GP fundholders are able to buy the help their patients need, but other GPs can use their influence to get round apparent blocks to medical services. Some hospitals, for example, which no longer provide acute beds have introduced GP beds. These are intended for short stays for people who temporarily cannot cope at home or who need respite care, but some GPs are using them to park their patients while waiting for an acute bed elsewhere (*see Chapter 11: Medical Care*).

The care network

As local authorities privatise more of their operations and as community care policies take effect, the network of people dealing with your ageing relatives becomes increasingly complex. You will come into contact with some of them as they give practical help; others remain in the background. Sometimes the public and private sector will overlap. For those who would rather act independently there is nothing to stop you bypassing local authorities and making your own arrangements. For those who are short of money and need to take advantage of subsidised or free services, however, it is worth making sure you have got the best on offer from your local council before you approach in a private capacity the agencies.

Independent care agencies

As community care expands, so independent care agencies proliferate. They divide into two main categories:

• **The charitable care agencies.** These are non-profit organisations which provide a service for members of the community.

• **The private care agencies.** These are commercial companies which provide services such as home helps or nurses at a commercial rate, sometimes under contract to a local authority. Example: Country Cousins (*See Chapter 5*)

What is happening in the 1990s is that these two categories are overlapping more and more. This is happening not just because private and public-sector home helps are bumping into each

COMMUNITY CARE

other at Great-Aunt Annie's house, but also because charities are having to turn more often to national or local government for funding.

Coordinating the independent agencies

As soon as a social services department has taken over your (or Great-Aunt Annie's) case, the key person you need to keep in touch with is their care manager. There should be no need to bother the GP or a health centre unless you have a medical condition that needs attention, because the care manager is the person who co-ordinates all the help that can be provided by the local authority and the outside care agencies it uses. You should not need to approach the independent agencies directly unless your care manager says you have reached the limits of what the social service department can do.

However, even this new strategy is changing. Although local authorities have always been able to charge clients for their services, some are beginning increase their prices and introduce more stringent means-tests for the people using local authority services. Social service departments appear to be privatising themselves. In other words, if Great-Aunt Annie can't prove she's on the £8,000 breadline , she may find herself having to pay for the care assistant to help her out of bed and bath her. At the moment her social service department is probably providing this service for a modest weekly flat fee, and the difference is effectively being paid by local taxpayers. If the council charges a market rate it will be paid twice over.

Finding out about agencies

If the local telephone directory yields nothing, you can get information about domiciliary care agencies in your area from:

Independent Health Care Association   Tel: 071-430 0537
22 Little Russell Street, London WC1A 2HT

United Kingdom Home Care Association   Tel: 0181-288 1551
22 Southway, Carshalton, Surrey SM5 4HWT

120

9

Surviving in your own home

Most people would rather be carried out of their own homes feet first than be moved into sheltered housing or a nursing home. Fortunately there is a lot that can be done to enable you to stay in your own home and keep your independence, and there are many individuals and organisations willing to provide the help, information and support to make this happen.

An Englishman's telecottage

The Englishman's home is, of course, his castle. If it is a real castle, retirement can be spent comfortably in one wing, with the butler standing by. But many couples, at some stage between the age of 50 and 70, sell their family homes and choose another one, either to realise some cash or to make their daily lives easier.

Choosing a home for later, quieter, life does not have to mean moving into sheltered housing in Eastbourne or a bungalow on

121

SURVIVING AT HOME

the golf course with a resident housekeeper. Rapidly changing technology will make life much easier for older people to cope well in their own homes in the next century.

Virtual shopping

Some of these changes are already noticeable. Communication is the obvious one. Telephones have become mobile, so slow-moving people can carry them around. Here already, and getting cheaper and more effective all the time, are video-conferencing systems that can be adapted to keep families in touch with ageing parents who live out of every-day reach. And the growth of telephone and 'virtual' shopping (where goods can be ordered by clicking a symbol on a TV screen) will be no cure for loneliness but will help people who cannot walk long distances or carry heavy bags.

On a simpler level, different types of 'aid-call' alarms can be bought from companies, hired from charities, or provided by your local authority social services. Recent advances in telecommunications can make a great difference to an older person, as help can be summoned in ways not possible 20 years ago.

Insulation and energy conservation equipment is improving, with the wider use of, for example, movement-triggered light bulbs, computer-controlled solar water heating and super-light-weight insulation materials. And developments in materials technology and small car design may make it easier in the next century for older people to get around.

Where to go

Behind the rose-trellised door of your 21st century last resting place, therefore, may be a 'telecottage' wired up with modems, cable TV, computer and video communication and control systems and alarms. A gruesome thought? Not necessarily. Even the simplest innovations can be useful.

Choosing where to spend your gloriously free years involves common-sense decisions and people tend to make the same types of choice as they get older. The usual choices are:

•**Place** Moving out of a city centre to a quieter area that is near to transport and good medical facilities. Moving from an isolat-

ed country house closer to the centre of a village, nearer to shops.
• **Size** Smaller, demanding less maintenance. Or split—house for
you, converted barn for visiting children, so that you will see
them without either generation being a strain on the other.

Repairs and adaptations

For those who are into their 70s but don't want to move, there is
a lot that can be done to adapt a house to make it easier to live in.
The main considerations for anyone planning to stay in their
own home are convenience and accessibility. Even if you are fit
now, it is worth considering the following points:

• The entrance to your home should be either level or gently
sloping and be close to your parking space, if you have one.

• Most essential rooms should be on the ground floor, and there
should be enough space downstairs to turn one of the rooms into
a bedroom if necessary.

• Windows should be easy to open and close, and also lockable.

• Other fittings, such as light switches, plugs and thermostats
should be set at a height usable by all, between 600mm and
1,200mm from the floor.

• A downstairs lavatory is essential, and it is a good idea if it is
is accessible in a wheelchair. Indeed all rooms should be large
enough to incorporate the turning circle of a wheelchair (this
needs a width of at least 1,500mm).

• If you have a downstairs lavatory already it is advisable to
check the room's structure and plumbing to make sure that a
shower can be fitted at a later date.

• Bathroom and lavatory walls should be checked to see if they
are capable of taking weight-bearing adaptations like hand-rails.
The bathroom design should provide easy access to the bath,
lavatory and wash basin, and its ceiling should be strong enough
to support a hoist.

• The house design should also make provision for a future stair
lift, and the stairs themselves should have a wide step or landing
half-way up to allow the home-owner to stop and have a
breather.

• Particular attention should be paid to good kitchen design,

SURVIVING AT HOME

with the emphasis on easily operated and accessible units and carefully positioned appliances. It should be possible to adapt existing kitchen units to meet individual requirements.

Planning for perfectionists

Only a tiny proportion of older people will ever need a ceiling hoist or stairlift, so for most people these guidelines err on the side of extreme caution. If you are hopelessly hypochondriac, however, or a perfectionist in your planning for old age, you can check any further structural guidelines with the Access Committee for England.

Specifications such as the following one for internal doorways are covered in greater detail in a free booklet called *Lifetime homes*, available on request from the Joseph Rowntree Foundation

---

MOVING HOUSE
If you are a local authority or housing association tenant and you are thinking about moving from one area to another, it might be worthwhile contacting H.O.M.E.S. to see if they can help you find somewhere nearer to your family and friends on their HOMESWAP register:
•H.O.M.E.S. (Housing Organisations Mobility and Exchange Services) , 26 Chapter Street, London SW1P 4ND
Tel. 0171 233 7077

• Internal doorways should have a clear opening width of no less than 750mm, with no less than 800mm for the front door, and hallways must be at least 900mm wide. If there is a radiator or similar obstruction in a hallway, then 750mm should be enough to allow easy movement. Getting around the house, however, can be made even easier if such obstructions are recessed. Corridor corners can cause problems to those in wheelchairs, and the corners can be chamfered if there is a 90° turn and the hallway is less than 900mm wide.

The Access Committee for England (ACE)   **Tel: 0171-250 0008**
12 City Forum, 250 City Road, London EC1V 8AF.

The Joseph Rowntree Foundation   **Tel: 01904-629 241**
The Homestead, 40 Water End, York Y03 6LP

And you can get full versions of these building requirements from :

Her Majesty's Stationery Office (HMSO)   **Tel: 0171-873 9090**
49 High Holborn, London WC1V 6HB, or;

Home improvement agencies

Adapting or repairing your home may seem a monumental task, but there are plenty of organisations which can provide practical help and financial support.

A word of warning: do not be seduced into spending large amounts of money on alterations such as widening doors unless you are pretty sure you are going to need it. And obviously, references supplied by builders need to be taken up—preferably by a personal phone call to a previous customer.

There is a growing network of home improvement agencies, usually called *Care & Repair* or *Staying Put*, which help the elderly to stay in their own homes by helping them tackle the otherwise overwhelming business of carrying out necessary repairs or adaptations.

Agencies like these will take clients through the whole process,

125

SURVIVING AT HOME

including sorting out finances—for instance, by arranging interest-only loans, applying for local authority grants or making applications to charities. Staff survey your home and help you to decide what work is necessary, provide a list of approved contractors and oversee the work from start to finish. Some agencies may employ a handyman who can can be hired at a reasonable rate to help with minor repairs or odd jobs.

The national coordinating body for home improvement agencies in England is Care & Repair Ltd. It can tell you about home improvement agencies in your area. Your local branch of Age Concern or your local authority social services department may also be able to help with addresses. The Anchor Housing Association also runs a *Staying Put* scheme.

CARE & REPAIR LTD

Care & Repair (England)   **Tel: 0115-979 9091**
Castle House, Kirtley Drive
Nottingham, NG7 1LD

Care & Repair Scotland   **Tel: 0141-248 7177**
Development Support Unit
Scottish Homes, Mercantile Chambers
53 Boswell Street, Glasgow G2 6TS

Care & Repair Cymru   **Tel: 01222-57628**
Norbury House, Norbury Road,
Cardiff, CF5 3AS

Care & Repair is the national coordinating body for the UK's 180 mainly publicly funded home improvement agencies—it receives 70 per cent of its funding from the Department of the Environment. As well as researching housing issues and influencing government policy, Care & Repair also acts as a support and training organisation for these government-subsidised home improvement agencies. Care & Repair can put you in touch with a home improvement agency in your area. •Among its publications is a free information guide for retired home-owners called *In good repair.*

SURVIVING AT HOME

ANCHOR GROUP

Anchor Group　　　　　　　　　　**Tel: 01865-311 511**
269a Banbury Road, Oxford OX2 7HU

Anchor is the largest provider of non-profit making housing and care services for older people in the UK. Anchor's *Staying put* service helps people who want to stay in their own homes but who find this difficult because their property needs to be repaired or adapted. The service will advise and help with grant applications, apply for interest-free loans, find suitable contractors and supervise work while it is carried out. *See also Chapter 10.*

Home renovation grants

Your local council can give grants to cover some or all of the cost of getting repair or adaptation work done. Some work, like installing an inside lavatory or repairing dangerous electrical wiring, qualifies for a *mandatory grant*. This means that your local council has to give you a grant if you qualify on financial grounds. As of 14 January 1994 the maximum *mandatory renovation grant* is £20,000. Other types of work may qualify for a discretionary grant, which means that the council decides if you are eligible for an award and, if you are, how much you will get.

Minor works grants

This grant is only available from the local authorities which choose to provide it. *Minor works grants* of up to £1,080 per application are available to homeowners, members of housing associations or private tenants over the age of 60 who are getting income support, council tax benefit, housing benefit or family credit. The council can pay up to a maximum of £3,240 on a single property over a three-year period. The size of the grant you receive depends on your income and savings.

Disabled facilities grants

There are also *disabled facilities grants* designed to help make the home of a disabled person more suitable for him or her to live in, and to help that person manage more independently. These grants cover all or part of the cost of adaptation work. As of 14 January 1994 the maximum *mandatory disabled facilities grant* was £20,000.

The renovation grants department of the local council will consult the social services department, and will usually arrange for an occupational therapist to assess your needs. However, occupational therapists employed by social service departments are usually very busy and you may have to wait a long time for a visit. If you are an outpatient at the local hospital you can ask if the hospital occupational therapist can help. If the assessment for a grant finds that your proposed improvements are necessary and appropriate to your needs and that any work is reasonable and practicable, given the age and condition of your property, then you will be eligible for a mandatory grant.

Means testing for grants

Your earnings and savings will be assessed when applying for any of these grants, and the result of this test of financial resources will dictate the size of the grant that is awarded. The test enables the local authority to work out how much you can afford to pay towards the cost of improving your home. The amount of grant you get—if any—will be the difference between the amount you are reckoned to be able to afford yourself and the total cost of the works which are eligible for a grant.

THE OCCUPATIONAL THERAPIST

Older people face problems ranging from stiff joints to the more serious effects of a stroke, heart condition or memory loss. Occupational therapists aim to help them overcome the effects of these disabilities so that they can continue living at home with as little dependence on relatives as possible. The occupational therapist is also the expert most often relied on by local authorities to advise on adaptations needed for people's homes. They not only help with adaptations and equipment, but give support to family carers and help with the treatment of older people. Treatment frequently focusses on helping people with everyday activities. This may mean teaching new ways of managing personal care and housework, like washing, dressing, cooking and shopping.

The means test calculates your average weekly income, "taking into acount the income you are reckoned to receive from any savings you have over £5,000". This is set against an assessment of your basic needs, which takes into account factors like your family status and any special needs, such as those relating to disability or old age. If you are on *income support* or your financial resources are below the means test standard, you will not have to contribute anything towards the cost of the work, as the full cost will be covered by the grant.

However if the local authority decides that your financial resources are above this means-test standard, part of your extra income is used to calculate the size of the contribution that the local authority reckons you are able to afford to pay for any improvements. This notional 'affordable loan' is then deducted from the cost of the works, and you will receive a grant to cover the remaining cost. The simple formula is: *amount of grant* equals *cost of work* minus *affordable loan*.

There are no hard and fast rules for these financial tests, as they are made by individual local authorities who use slightly differing criteria when assessing grant applications. This test is complex and the above description is only an indication of how it works. You will not have to repay a *disabled facilities grant*.

•For information on what you can and cannot apply for and the procedures involved, the Department of the Environment publishes a free booklet: *House renovation grants*. You can also ask for this from your local council's renovation grants department or your nearest housing advice centre or Citizens Advice Bureau.

Community care grants

If you are on income support and are receiving benefit, you may be able to get a *community care grant* from the Department of Social Security's *social fund*. These are intended primarily to help elderly or disabled people live independently in the community. The *social fund* helps people cover the sudden expenses that they cannot meet from their regular income, such as urgent improvements or repairs to their home.

•For an application form you should get in touch with your local Social Security office and ask for form SF 300, or if you want to

SURVIVING AT HOME

find out more about *social fund* payments get leaflet SB16 *A guide to the social fund*. The amount of *community care grant* you get is affected if you have more than £500 of savings or other capital, or £1,000 if you are 60 or over. However when applying it is important to remember that there is no right to help from this fund, and that there is a limited amount of money available.

Home energy efficiency scheme

Insulation can help to cut down on bills as well as keeping you warmer. Anyone who is 60 or over who rents or owns their home can get a government grant to cover the cost of draught-proofing doors and windows and insulating the hot water tank and the loft—if it has less than two inches of insulation. The laws relating to the provision of grants are in Part Eight of the 1989 *Local Government Act*. If you are under 60 you can apply only if you are receiving *income support, housing benefit, council tax benefit, family credit, disability working allowance* or *disability allowance*. The scheme is run by:

Energy Action Grants Agency Tel: Freephone 0800-181 667
FREEPOST   **Minicom (for the deaf): 0191-233 1054**
PO Box 1NG, Newcastle upon Tyne, NE99 2RP

If you are considering applying for a grant it is important to contact the renovation grants section at your local council *before* you start any work. Whatever work is to be done it is a good idea to employ a quailified architect or surveyor to plan and oversee the work (if you do get a grant their fees can be included in the cost of the works). Your local authority may be able to give you a list of local architects and surveyors, or you could contact the Royal Institute of British Architects (RIBA) or the Royal Institution of Chartered Surveyors (RICS). The Centre for Accessible Environments can supply helpful information relating to design for elderly and disabled people, as can the Disabled Living Foundation.

Royal Institute of British Architects (RIBA)   Tel: 0171-580 5533
66 Portland Place, London W1N 4AD

SURVIVING AT HOME

Royal Institution of Chartered Surveyors   **Tel: 0171-222 7000**
12 Great George Street, London SW1P 3AD

Centre for Accessible Environments   **Tel: 0171-357 8182**
60 Gainsford Street, London SE1 2NY

Disabled Living Foundation   **Tel: 0171-289 6111**
380-384 Harrow Road, London W9 2HU

Before deciding on the cost of the works eligible for a house renovation grant your local authority will normally ask for two written building estimates. Here it is advisable to use a builder who belongs to a trade association which operates a guarantee scheme like those run by the Building Employers Federation and the Federation of Master Builders. Most home improvement agencies employ a technical officer who can help choose the best builder for the job from a list of local member firms.

Building Employers Confederation   **Tel: 0171-580 5588**
82 New Cavendish Street, London W1M 8AD

Federation of Master Builders   **Tel: 0171-242 7583**
14-15 Great James Street, London WC1N 3DP

Assessments

If you have problems coping at home you can contact your local authority social services department for advice and help. You are entitled to get a *service assessment* (for example, for help with bathing and meals on wheels) and/or an *equipment assessment* (for example, for an alarm system), and you should expect the local authority to provide essential services under the terms of the 1990 *Community Care Act*.

Your assessment for services will usually be carried out by a domiciliary care manager, but if you are disabled it is likely that the assessment will be made by an occupational therapist. For more details see *Chapter 8: Social Services and Community Care.*

131

SURVIVING AT HOME

Equipment

Although equipment is frequently not the solution to a person's problems, an occupational therapist can tell you what useful aids to living are available. This can include, for example, tap-turners which are braille-marked for blind people and can be are fitted to ordinary taps to make them easier to turn.

The RNID (Royal National Institute for Deaf people) has a company (Sound Advantage) which provides listening aids and alarms for those who are deaf or hard-of-hearing. Similarly the RNIB (Royal National Institute for the Blind) has equipment for those who are blind or partially sighted.

Commercial companies produce a wide range of other aids, like wheelchairs, sticks, commodes and specially adapted cutlery to make eating easier for those who have restricted wrist movement or arthritis. There are also 22 government-funded Disabled Living Centres throughout the UK where equipment for elderly or disabled people and their carers is demonstrated.

•Useful reading

Equipment to aid daily living, Invaluable factsheet produced by The Carers National Association, giving information on where to get equipment.

Equipment and Services for Disabled People (Booklet HB6) produced by the department of Social Security (DSS). You can get a copy of this by writing to or phoning your local DSS office.

Carers National Association   **Tel: 0171-490 8818**
20/25 Glasshouse Yard
London EC1A 4JS

Royal National Institute for Deaf People   **Tel: 0171-387 8033**
105 Gower Street, London WC1

Royal National Institute for the Blind   **Tel: 0171-388 1266**
224 Great Portland Street, London W1N 6AA

Stairlifts

A stairlift is, at its simplest, rather like a seat on an escalator that glides upstairs and parks you at the top, or like a smooth-running ski-lift. Stairlifts and lifts can be absolutely essential for people who have a heart condition or are unable to walk except with support. Before buying the stairlift of one's dreams, however, bear in mind that they are expensive to install and plan that it should be in use for at least five years. In other words, it is not sensible for Great-Uncle Archie and Great-Aunt Annie to put a stairlift into their house if they decide in two year's time that will be necessary to have both their bedrooms downstairs.

If a stairlift makes sense long-term, you can get advice from your local social services department about suitability, safety, and installation and maintenance costs. Each stairlift is different, as it is tailored both to the customer and to his or her staircase. Stannah Stairlifts suggests that prices start at around £1,980 for installation on a simple straight staircase, and at roughly £3,900 for a complex or curved staircase. Companies which install stairlifts are listed below:

Stannah Stairlifts Ltd.　　　　　　**Tel: 01264-332 244**
Watt Close, East Portway
Andover, Hampshire SP10 3SD

Brooks Stairlifts Ltd.　　　　　　**Tel: 01522-500 288**
Westminster Industrial Estate
Station Road, North Hykeham, Lincoln LN6 3QY

Selflift Chair Co.　　　　　　**Tel: 01905-778 116**
Mahler House, 130 Worcester Road
Droitwich Spa, Worcs. WR9 8AN

Gimson Stairlifts　　　　　　**Tel: 0800-622 251**
62 Boston Road, Leicester LE4 1AZ

SURVIVING AT HOME

Beds and chairs

These can vary from the sturdy, well-designed and comfortable furniture that is available at normal shops to specialist lifting chairs, or beds with electrically-operated back or foot rests that can, for example, raise a limb that needs to be kept horizontal because of blood circulation problems. Specialist chairs include commodes for those who need to go to the lavatory in the night but cannot get there.

As with stairlifts, most specialised beds and chairs are made to order, so the price will depend on the size and specification of the item. Most companies will discuss the customer's needs before giving a firm quotation. Powered chairs (that lift you to your feet, for example) and beds are not particularly cheap: a powered seat lift chair costs in the region of £675, and a powered reclining/lifting chair roughly £995. A double size bed with solo control costs an estimated £2,173 and one with dual control £3,212. Some chair and commode manufacturers include:

Adjustamatic Beds   **Tel: 01293-783 837**
2 Lumley Road, Horley
Surrey RH6 7RJ

Back-Care (Chairs)   **Tel: 01924-464 809**
Victoria Road, Dewsbury
W. Yorks WF13 2AB

Theraposture Ltd (Beds & Chairs)   **Tel: 01985-847 788**
Warminster Business Park
Bath Road, Warminster, Wilts BA12 8PE

Recliners Unlimited (Beds & Chairs)   **Tel: 01443-229 119**
20 Cowbridge Road
Pontyclun, Mid-Glamorgan CF7 9EE

Bathroom appliances

There is a wide variety of handrails and special floorings which can be put into a bathroom to prevent slipping or falling, which most often happens when you get in or out of the bath. It is possible to reduce this danger further by adding a bath seat to an existing bath, or by installing a specialised bath with built-in seating.

Powered bath seats go one step further by allowing the user to lower himself or herself into the bath and out again safely and with even less effort. However a powered bath lift can cost around £440, and this does not include the additional £90 for the hand controller.

Similarly, there are raised lavatory seats available to help those who have difficulty standing up and sitting down. Some of these seats have a chair-like lifting action, and others have back rests and/or arm supports. If these fittings are not enough, special support frames can be installed around the lavatory to give additional support. Once in the bathroom there are many items that can be used to make personal care easier, like a toothpaste tube holder and squeezer, long-handled bath brushes, hairbrushes and combs (see *Gadgets* on the next page).

Parker Bath Developments   **Tel: 01425-622 287**
Stem Lane, New Milton
Hants. BH25 5NN

Dolphin Special Needs Bathrooms   **Tel: 01905-748 500**
Bromwich Road, Worcester WR2 4BD

Aqua Therapy Limited   **Tel: 0161-929 9191**
Grosvenor House, Grafton Street
Altringham, Cheshire WA14 1BR

Appollo Baths   **Tel: 01794-511 555**
Appollo House, The Quadrangle,
Abbey Park, Romsey, Hants SO51 9AQ

SURVIVING AT HOME

Gadgets

There is a bewildering array of useful gadgets to make everyday tasks more manageable. The following items give only an indication of what can be found:

A whole range of long-handled equipment, like shoe horns, sock and stocking pullers, pincers for picking things up off the floor, and a door and window opener that enables those with a restricted reach to open door lever handles and other catches.

For those who lack strength in the hands and wrists there are tap and key turners, tin and jar openers, a kettle-tipper and jug-pourer, cutlery with contoured handles or grip tubing, a hand strap to make picking up and holding telephones easier, and a 'plug pull', a self-adhesive plastic T-piece that sticks to the back of a standard plug, and provides leverage for removing an electric plug from the socket.

A 'walker trolley' can make moving things around the house a lot easier. These 'things' might include needle-threaders, leg-rests and pillows, non-slip mats for cups and plates to go on non-slip trays, and pill dispensers and tablet splitters. These products and many others can be found in, and usually ordered from, the catalogues of the companies listed below.

Chester Care   **Tel: 01623-757 955**
Sidings Road, Low Moor Estate,
Kirkby-in-Ashfield, Notts. NG17 7JZ

Keep Able   **Tel: 01933-679 426**
7 Fleming Close, Park Farm
Wellingborough, Northants. NN8 6UF

Home and Comfort   **Tel: 01789-470 055**
PO Box 25, Wellesbourne
Warwick CV35 9TY

Smith and Nephew Homecraft Ltd.   **Tel: 01252-714 182**
Farnham Trading Estate, Farnham, Surrey GU9 9NQ

Telephones

Improved equipment and support services can enable anyone to use a telephone. There are many aids available to people who have impaired mobility, vision or hearing. British Telecom, with the help of the RNIB, can send copies of telephone bills in braille or can phone you and read out the details of the bill before posting it. Much of the information provided by the RNIB and BT is available on tape as well. There are textphones available for people who are profoundly deaf, and because calls made with this equipment take much longer and the bills are therefore much higher, the RNID runs a *Text user rebate scheme* providing a 60 per cent rebate of the call charge portion of the bill up to a maximum or £160. For further details of this scheme you can write to:

Text Users Rebate Scheme   Tel: 0151-494 1000
Pauline Ashley House   Textphone: 0800-500 888
Ravenside Retail Park
Speke Road, Liverpool L24 8QB

Also situated at Pauline Ashley House is *Typetalk*, the national telephone relay service. This enables textphone users to ring or receive calls from hearing people. Calls are made by a relay operator who types the hearing person's reply which appears on the screen of the non-hearing person. As with the *Text users rebate scheme*, *Typetalk* is run by the RNID with funds from BT. The Partially Sighted Society of Great Britain can provide a large print list of national dialling codes, and the RNIB customer services department have a braille guide to residential telephone charges as well as lists of dialling codes.

There are cordless phones and answering machines for those who have difficulty moving around the house and phones with luminous push buttons for those with partial sight loss, amplifiers for those with partial hearing loss, and flashing lights and vibrating indicators for profoundly deaf people. After you have used all this equipment you can get large-print bills.

SURVIVING AT HOME

The 1970 *Chronically Sick and Disabled Persons Act* requires local authorities to assess the needs of disabled people for help with the costs of installing and renting a telephone and any special equipment that may be necessary. For more information a fact sheet, *Help with telephones*, is available from Age Concern on receipt of a stamped addressed envelope.

• You can get more details of the aids and services that BT have on offer by dialling 0800 800 150.

• A freephone (0800 66 55 44) *health helpline* has been set up through the Patient's Charter to provide confidential information on common diseases and ailments, NHS services, waiting times, local Patient's Charter standards, complaints procedures and how to stay healthy. The lines are open between 10am and 5pm, Monday to Friday.

Alarm telephone systems

Older people who live alone or who find it difficult to get out and about may appreciate the security of knowing that they can contact someone in an emergency. All you need to fit an alarm is a plug-in telephone socket and a thirteen-amp power point within six feet of each other; preferably on the same wall to avoid the possibility of tripping over trailing leads.

The alarm works like a normal telephone. If it is triggered it will automatically dial a 24-hour emergency centre. To trigger the alarm all you need to do is press a button either on the telephone or on a pendant that is usually continuously worn around your neck. This portable trigger has a range of at least 25 yards.

ALARMS.
A survey of alarm system users carried out in 1990 by the Harris Research Centre for Help the Aged found that :
88% lived alone
54% were over 80
61% were not fully mobile
86% felt safer as a result of having an alarm unit
Most of the 10% who had used the unit in an emergency had no-one else they could have called.

SURVIVING AT HOME

When you push the button and your call is received by the emergency centre your details will be listed. These details contain information that you have previously supplied, like your name and address, medical history, doctor and local friends or relatives who have the keys to your property so that the emergency services do not have to break in.

Emergency procedures

The alarm unit also has a microphone and a loudspeaker built into it to allow the caller to talk to the control centre staff even if he or she cannot reach the telephone. However if the staff are unable to speak to you they will assume that it is an emergency and send the emergency services or a warden.

You can get an alarm either from your local authority, a commercial firm, or through a charity. There are over three hundred alarm schemes run by local authority housing or social services departments, and getting an alarm from your local authority is usually the cheapest option. Some local authorities rent or lease alarms, others sell the unit and charge an annual monitoring fee of anything between £35 and £75 a year. If your local authority does not run an alarm service another nearby authority may be prepared to link an alarm that you have bought independently to their emergency centre. The Disabled Living Foundation has a comprehensive list of alarm systems.

Help the Aged Community Alarms Department can help with funding for an alarm unit for elderly people who cannot afford to provide their own. An alarm unit can cost anything between £230 and over £300. Indeed in the seven years that Help the Aged has been running its Community Alarms Programme, the charity has provided over 20,000 alarms.

•For advice on how to get a Community alarm for yourself you can call the Help the Aged freephone information and advice service *Seniorline* on 0800 289 404. The lines are open between 10am and 4pm, Monday to Friday. Or you can write to the :

Community Alarms Department   **Tel: 0171-253 0253**
Help the Aged, 16 - 18 St. James's Walk
London EC1R OBE

SURVIVING AT HOME

The Disabled Living Foundation   **Tel: 0171-289 6111**
380/384 Harrow Road
London W9 2HU

Home help services

Home helps provide practical day to day help with chores like cleaning and shopping. However some helpers will not undertake anything more than light household duties. Some local authorities no longer offer help with cleaning, although other social services departments still may provide a laundry service for people with incontinence, or those who can-not manage their laundry for any other reason. There are a number of private agencies which recruit and place living-in companions and daily or longer-term nurses or care workers.

In order to provide continuous help, many agencies operate a rota system with carers working alternate weekly or fortnightly shifts each month. Each agency has its own system for placing staff, and the experience and level of care provided by their employees can vary considerably, as can the cost. The United Kingdom Home Care Association has lists of member agencies and others in the UK:

United Kingdom Home Care Association   **Tel: 0181-770 3658**
42 Banstead Road
Carshalton Beeches, Surrey SM5 3NW

For further help you could contact Counsel and Care. This charity gives advice on problems such as finding the right care home and how to negotiate the labyrinthine procedures of the social services. Counsel and Care also has some grant aid to give away each year to support older people in or at home, but like many other charities the emphasis is shifting to giving advice about how to access other sources of financial support. The charity holds databases on independent care homes in London (and will help you to find a suitable one), home-care agencies and grant-making charities.

SURVIVING AT HOME

- Counsel and Care publishes useful factsheets (free to individual enquirers with a large SAE), including: *A guide to community care choices for older people, What to look for in a private or voluntary registered home,* and *Help at home.*

Counsel and Care   **Tel: 0171-485 4513**
Twyman House, 16 Bonny Street
London NW1 9PG

Meals

Most 'meals on wheels' are organised either by the local authority or by local Age Concern or WRVS groups. A range of diets can be catered for, including vegetarian and kosher. Some provide a freezer for people at home and deliver frozen meals that you can heat up and eat when you want to. Meals on wheels may be offered any number of days per week, but usually the service covers Monday to Friday. What you get will depend on how your needs are assessed and on the resources of your local authority.

Women's Royal Voluntary Service (WRVS)   **Tel: 0171-416 0146**
234 to 244 Stockwell Road
London SW9 9SP

Virtual shopping

The development of virtual shopping (shopping via a computer screen) will help oldies to buy what they need from a well-worn armchair. If you are plugged into the Internet via a modem linking your computer to a telephone you will be able, for example, to surf into the BarclaySquare 'virtual shopping mall', where you will be able open the door to different 'virtual stores' like Sainsburys by clicking with a computer mouse. With a few more clicks you will be able to choose the products you want, key in your credit card number, and have the goods delivered to your door.

•BarclaySquare (Internet address): http://www.itl.net/barclaysquare/

SURVIVING AT HOME

Mail order

If you are due to become a 21st-century oldie, you may do your shopping by cybersurfing. But for the time being there is nothing to beat mail order. Even food can be ordered by mail: as well as finding out what is on offer from the traditional big stores you can try some specialised newcomers. Here is the address of a company (not unconnected with this book's publisher) that will mail you superb coffee, olive oil, pink peppercorns or other specialities from a catalogue that makes you feel you are eating on a Tuscan hillside:

Morel Bros., Cobbett & Son　　　　　　**Tel: 0171-346 0046**
Unit 7, 129 Coldharbour Lane　　　　　　Fax: 0171-346 0033
London SE5 9NY

For home-sitting services, see *Chapter 6: Staying busy*, and for details of the state benefits you can get which may help to contribute to your care, see *Chapter 7: Money*.

Going into a home

Nursing homes are, of course, not home at all. That's one reason why the prospect of going into one fills people with dread. Another is that they cost a lot of money, so that the longer you stay alive in one of them, the poorer you get. Then you have to sell your house to meet the bills, then you have no home to go if you recover, and nothing to leave to your family. Are your prospects for old age really as bad as this? If you think so, turn back to CHAPTER 4: 50 PLUS and think about keeping fit before you read on. Financial planning is covered in CHAPTER 7: MONEY.

Last staging post?

Increased life expectancy means that many people who a generation ago would expect to retire at 65 and die in their 70s can now expect to retire at 65 and live into their 80s or 90s. This may be good news for the fit and well-off with helpful children to hand, but it is bad news for someone who is already 80 and faces a decade of steady deterioration.

Today's over-50s are worried that they may survive financially for up to 20 years after retirement, only to have to be admitted to a nursing home for the last ten. Who will pay? Will Great-Uncle Archie and Great-Aunt Annie really have to sell the

RESIDENTIAL & NURSING HOMES

NUMBERS

According to Laing & Buisson, experts on the market in care for elderly people, the number of people in care homes and long-stay hospitals dropped in 1994 for the first time. Does this mean the elderly and disabled are now being better looked after at home?

	April 1993 (Community Care)	April 1994 One year later	Change
Private residential homes	152,000	150,000	(-1.32%)
Private nursing homes	159,000	164,000	(+1.03%)
Local authority homes	84,000	77,000	(-8.34%)
NHS long-stay beds	56,000	51,000	(-8.93%)
	451,000	**442,000**	**(-2.00%)**

Care of Elderly People Market Survey: Laing & Buisson, 38 Georgiana Street, London NW1 0EB. £285.

honeysuckled cottage that they assumed they would pass on to their son—so that they can pay nursing home fees? If the state will not pay Archie's fees until he is down to his last £8,000, son Fred will have nothing to look forward to when he in turn retires.

With 10 million home owners in the electorate, this issue has been recognised as a political hot potato. In April 1995 Prime Minister John Major announced that his next election manifesto would include policies to guarantee that parents could pass on their homes to their children when they die. The four-point draft plan included schemes for leasing a room in a nursing home instead of renting one; creating a tax-privileged 'care bond'; encouraging care insurance with tax breaks; and raising the threshold for inheritance tax. Whatever happens, saving for old age is back in fashion. It is even being argued that it should be made compulsory. Unfortunately for some people it is already too late for that.

Leaving home

There are several stages between surviving in your own home and going 'permanently' into a nursing home. Any of these moves: into sheltered housing, a residential care home, or a nursing home, can be triggered by coming out of hospital after illness

RESIDENTIAL & NURSING HOMES

and become a permanent move. Equally any stage can be temporary or can be skipped, and the early stages can be made to last
as long as possible.

Community care and going into a home

The 1990 *NHS and Community Care Act*, as already explained, is
changing the way Britain looks after its old. Before the Act anyone who met criteria set by the Department of Social Security

---

D.I.Y. NURSING HOME

*Archie is now too senile to look after himself and Annie has a very
weak heart. By an extraordinary stroke of luck, they have just won a
six-figure sum on the National Lottery. To stay at Honeysuckle
Cottage they would need £35,000 (about £350 a week for two years
including interest) to be spent on alterations, including a new
downstairs bathroom and a stairlift. Then they would have to have
two full-time nurses working in shifts, with a part-time helper to fill
in the gaps and do odd jobs, costing £650 a week. That's £1,000 a
week, more than two rooms in a good nursing home, but they would
keep the cottage. If Great-Uncle Archie's cousin 'Buffy' Musket
(also a one-time soldier, now recovering from a stroke) joins the
family, however, the DIY solution begins to look worthwhile.*

*•Advice: staff and supplies still need to be managed by a clued-up
relative. Own rooms with TV for each person and communal
dining-room, just like a real nursing home.*

RESIDENTIAL & NURSING HOMES

(DSS) showing that they were elderly, poor and unable to cope in their own homes was moved into an institutional home and the bills were paid by central government in the shape of the DSS. During the 1980s there was a boom in residential care homes and nursing homes as beds were filled. By 1994, an astonishing 71 per cent of all residential and nursing home beds were filled with people whose fees were being paid by the state.

The government had already realised that a lot of money was being wasted by putting people into institutions when they did not really need to be there and would have been much happier staying at home. Why not take care to the people at home instead of taking people to the care home?

The *NHS and Community Care Act* did this by handing responsibility from central government to local government. As explained in Chapter 8, local authorities now have to make every effort to support frail elderly people with services in their own homes rather than pay for them to go into a nursing home.

Home care?

The community care revolution is bringing good results and bad. On the positive side, older people are now less likely to be moved into a residential or nursing home without their needs being assessed properly first. Financially it also makes sense to stay in the family home as long as possible. Domiciliary (home) care agencies are also expected become more efficient as demand for their services expands and new private agencies are started up. At present, however, home care services as organised by social service departments tend to be patchy and family back-up may be needed. *See Chapter 8.*

Or sheltered housing?

A half-way step between surviving at home and going into a care home is to move into sheltered housing. This term covers a range of houses and flats which are specially designed for elderly people, with varying degrees of porterage and protection.

146

RESIDENTIAL & NURSING HOMES

THE INHERITANCE DILEMMA

A painful dilemma arises when someone has only a few thousand pounds of savings left but needs to go into a care home. If he is one of a couple, and his wife wants to stay in the family home, it cannot be sold to pay care home fees. But if he or she is alone and the house will become empty, it may have to be sold and the proceeds used to pay nursing home fees before a local authority will agree to take final responsibility to pay

The sale proceeds may be claimed by a local authority even if the house has already been passed on to a relative within six months before the sale, if a local authority can prove it was done in the expectation that nursing home fees would soon have to be paid.

• Trust If family relationships are good and your children are self-sufficient, you can leave your house in trust to them while you are still healthy. This should not be done unless you have other funds in reserve, and the terms of the trust can guarantee that you will be able to live there until you die. You may prefer to hold on to your house until you have to pay for a private nursing home of your own choice. Take good legal advice first, because there are pitfalls.

Or a care home?

A last resort for most people. They simply don't want to leave home. Even worse, the family home may have to be sold to pay later for nursing home fees. But for those who can no longer cope, even with children, neighbours and cleaners to help, the decision is no longer whether to go into a home, but what type of home to go into and how to finance it—for example, by buying an annuity. *See Chapter 7.*

Types of care home

There are two types of 'care home': a residential care home (which used to be known as an 'old people's home') and a nursing home. Residential homes vary in style from small homes like boarding houses to quite grand ones with individual rooms, and there are three times as many residential homes as nursing homes. Nursing homes are equipped and staffed to give nursing

147

RESIDENTIAL & NURSING HOMES

> **WELCOME TO ZIMMERLAND**
> *People prefer to stick with their peer group, and elderly tenants of a care home in Santa Barbara, California, did not want their standards lowered by having to mix with even wobblier geriatrics. To avoid relegation, the inmates had to prove to the tenants' association that they could get from the dining-room door to the dining table without help. Soon they were seen crouching at the doorway, poised for a long vault to the dining table without sticks or Zimmer frames. Who says oldies have no motivation?*

care. There is also a third, the dual-registration home, which combines the first two categories.

The residential care home

First the residential home. This is a home for people who are elderly and frail, but are not normally likely to need nursing care: the simplest distinction between a residential home and a nursing home.

Whether a residential home takes disabled people depends on how well it is equipped—for example with special baths. One residential home may be willing to take on a severely incontinent person while another is not. When deciding whether to admit your ageing parent, the residential or nursing home manager will be guided by the social worker's assessment (if the local authority is going to pay the fees) and its own separate assessment for a private admission. Similarly, your parent's choice of nursing or residential home should be made after discussing the various options available with the same social worker. Again, social workers do not have to be involved if an elderly person is to pay his own way.

However choosing a residential home is not solely a matter of 'options'. It is as much to do with kindness, attention and trust as with equipment and surroundings. It is also important that the home's oldies (often affectionately known as 'inmates') are the type who might get on with your aged parent. According to Laing & Buisson, average residential care home fees for the financial year 1994-1995 were £234 a week.

RESIDENTIAL & NURSING HOMES

The nursing home

All the above applies, but a nursing home can be equipped to look after people with almost any condition that does not need continuous hospital treatment. It should have at least one fully qualified state registered nurse on duty 24 hours a day. According to Laing & Buisson, average weekly fees for the financial year 1994-1995 were £324.

•Information and advice

There are several sources of information and advice to help you find out about local residential care homes and nursing homes, and you do not have to go through the social services department of a local authority if you do not wish to and you are able to pay. These are listed at the end of the detailed sections on *residential homes* and *nursing homes* further on in this chapter.

Sheltered housing

First it is worth taking a look at types of housing that fall between one's own home and a nursing home, known as sheltered housing. The Elderly Accommodation Council has identified 500,000 sheltered homes, including almshouses and Abbeyfield Society type homes, in the United Kingdom.

Independent retirement housing

This category of housing covers bungalows, cottages or flats designed for the active retired or elderly person. Some may have

---

WHAT TO LOOK FOR IN SHELTERED HOUSING

- How easy is access (including wheelchair access)?
- Is it close to shops, doctor, dentist, bank, library and post office?
- Is there good public transport nearby?
- What communal facilities are there? For example, is there a communal laundry if kitchens are too small for a washing machine?
- Is there a room or flatlet for visitors to stay overnight, and do you have to hire it?
- Do they allow pets?
- Is car parking available?

an alarm system linked to a central control. A development may have a group of retirement units or just one or two, and there are unlikely to be communal facilities. Independent retirement housing is available to rent or buy through private developers or housing associations, trusts or societies.

Types of sheltered housing

The quality of sheltered housing is usually high and sheltered housing is increasingly being provided by housing associations. Choosing between the many types of sheltered housing available however, and knowing what sorts of facilities and services each provides can be a confusing business. Terms such as 'extra-care', 'Abbeyfield-style' or 'very-sheltered' give little indication of what they mean in practice: buyers have to shop around.

The move to community care means that many sheltered housing schemes are beginning to offer higher levels of care to their residents when they become less able to look after themselves, but do not want to move to a residential home. Sometimes sheltered housing is provided alongside a nursing home, with a future move in mind. It can also be provided by having 'extra-care' wings in standard schemes, or by developing 'care teams' in association with local social services departments.

Wardens of many sheltered housing schemes are now being trained as 'care managers' who are able to assess the needs of each resident and arrange for the appropriate care or services. The emphasis in sheltered housing is on privacy and independence with support and there are now many alternatives to moving into a residential home. Some of the different types of sheltered housing are described below.

Sheltered housing: safe and sound?

A sheltered housing scheme is a group of self-contained flats or bungalows which have communal facilities, an alarm system, and a warden. They are designed for older people who can look after themselves but want the security of having a warden on site to offer support or help in an emergency. When the warden is off duty an alarm system provides back-up. Communal facilities will be different in each scheme, but frequently include a com-

RESIDENTIAL & NURSING HOMES

mon room and communal laundry, with perhaps a guest room for visitors. Sheltered housing is usually provided unfurnished and is available for rent or sale through local authorities, housing asscociations, trusts or societies, or through some voluntary and charitable organisations.

Extra-sheltered housing

These schemes (or ones with similar names, such as very-sheltered, extra-care or supportive care) are intended for frailer older people who needs a higher level of care, but wish to keep their privacy and independence. They offer the same type of accommodation as standard sheltered housing—self-contained flats or bungalows with communal facilities and a warden—but with a much wider range of support and services. A warden is usually on duty 24 hours a day. Extra-sheltered housing is available on the same basis as sheltered housing.

Leasehold for the elderly

'Leasehold for the Elderly' schemes are designed for elderly people who would like to buy a sheltered home but who have only a small amount of capital and a limited income. The schemes are run by housing associations which build sheltered housing developments on a shared-ownership basis for people aged 55 or over, on a 99-year lease. Buyers have a choice of buying a 25 per cent, 50 per cent or 75 per cent share. Those buying a quarter or half share must pay rent in addition to the purchase price.

If a leaseholder wishes to sell, he is normally able to sell to anyone over the age of 55, though the housing association may have the option of nominating someone from its waiting list. There may be waiting lists for these schemes, which are said to be very much in demand. The schemes are financed and monitored by the Housing Corporation, the government agency which regulates housing associations. For the addresses of their regional offices, who will be able to give you details of schemes in your area contact:

The Housing Corporation   **Tel: 0171-393 2000**
149 Tottenham Court Road, London W1P 0BN

151

RESIDENTIAL & NURSING HOMES

Abbeyfield-style accommodation

These are bedsitting-rooms, some with en-suite facilities and kitchenette, in a family-sized house. At least one meal a day is provided and there is a communal lounge and dining room. Residents are expected to get their own breakfast and care for their rooms and personal laundry. See the **Abbeyfield Society** entry in *Chapter 5* for more information. Abbeyfield-style accommodation is available for rent (weekly), mainly through the voluntary and charity sector.

Almshouses

Almshouses were the earliest form of charitably-funded sheltered accommodation for elderly people: the oldest was founded in York in 1000 AD and many are still on their original 12th or 13th century sites. Today there are about 2,300 groups of almshouses in the UK, which provide around 26,000 homes for elderly people. Some offer high levels of care, but two-thirds are units for independent people and frequently have a resident warden. Almshouses are available for rent only. Most have eligibility requirements, either geographical or requiring some past association with a trade, profession or company.

•*Information*   You can get information about almshouse charities in your area from the **Housing or Social Services Department** of your local authority or your local **Citizen's Advice Bureau**. Or the **Almshouse Association** will provide you with a list of almshouses in your area. The **Elderly Accommodation Council** includes almshouses on its database.

Adult placement schemes

These 'foster' schemes for older people who can no longer cope on their own allows them to live with carers as part of the family. Carers are paid a fee for providing care and full board, and the person placed may be assessed for a financial contribution.

•*Contact*   Your local social services department, or your local branch of Age Concern may be able to tell you if a scheme exists in your area.

RESIDENTIAL & NURSING HOMES

Sheltered housing organisations

These are some of the organisations involved in provided sheltered homes, general housing for the elderly and the services that go with them:

THE ABBEYFIELD SOCIETY

The Abbeyfield Society   **Tel: 01727-857 536**
Abbeyfield House, 53 Victoria Street
St Albans, Herts, AL1 3UW

Abbeyfield Societies provide sheltered housing in 'supportive homes'. The homes are set up and run by local volunteers. The Abbeyfield philosophy balances privacy with 'caring support', involving residents in the life of the community. An Abbeyfield house is typically a family-sized house for 8-12 people with a resident housekeeper, call alarm systems, specialist facilities and support from local volunteers. Residents are given two cooked meals a day but prepare their own breakfasts. Private rooms are let unfurnished so that residents can bring their own furniture, and many have en-suite facilities. While the homes are designed for the more active elderly person (residents are expected to look after their own rooms), Abbeyfield Societies now run about 60 'extra care' houses or wings and two nursing homes. However priority for these is given to those already living in an Abbeyfield house. There are about 1,000 Abbeyfield houses nationwide; generally preference is given to local people or those with local connections.

THE ALMSHOUSE ASSOCIATION

The Almshouse Association   **Tel: 01344-52922**
Billingbear Lodge, Wokingham, Berks. RG11 5R

The Almshouse Association can provide lists of locally based almshouses.

RESIDENTIAL & NURSING HOMES

ANCHOR GROUP

Anchor Group　　　　　　　　　　**Tel: 01865-311 511**
269a Banbury Road, Oxford OX2 7HU

Anchor is the largest provider of non-profit making housing and care services for older people in the country. Through the Anchor Housing Association it operates 650 rental sheltered housing schemes, and care teams are being developed with local authority services to make these schemes more accessible to frailer elderly people. Anchor says that in its residential and nursing care schemes, the emphasis is on privacy, independence and dignity, with all residents having their own en-suite flats. Another part of the Anchor Group is the Guardian Housing Association which develops and manages sheltered housing units for sale.

COUNSEL AND CARE

Counsel and Care　　　　　　　**Tel: 0171-485 1550**
Twyman House　　　　　Advice Line: 0171-485 1566
16 Bonny Street　　　　　　　(10.30am-4.00pm)
London NW1 9PG

Counsel and Care operates a telephone and postal service giving advice on such problems as finding the right care home and how to negotiate with social services. A certain amount of grant aid is given each year to support older people in care or at home, but increasingly the emphasis is shifting to providing information and advice on how to get hold of other sources of financial support. Counsel and Care holds databases on independent care homes in Greater London (and will help to find a suitable one), or home care agencies and grant-making charities. Publications include a range of useful factsheets (free to individual enquirers with large SAE) including *A guide to community care choices for older people* and *What to look for in a private or voluntary registered home*. See also Counsel and Care entry in *Chapter 5*.

RESIDENTIAL & NURSING HOMES

ELDERLY ACCOMMODATION COUNCIL

The Elderly Accommodation Council   **Tel: 0181-995 8320**
46A Chiswick High Road   0181-742 1182
London W4 1SZ

The Elderly Accommodation Council aims to provide easily accessible information to elderly people seeking suitable accommodation. Its computerised national register covers all types of accommodation in the charity, private and local authority sectors, including retirement housing (sheltered and independent, for rent and for sale), Abbeyfield-style accommodation, almshouses, residential care homes, nursing homes and terminal hospices. Registered charity.

•**How EAC can help:** EAC operates an information service on the types of accommodation listed above and an advice service on sources of top-up funding for care costs. The accommodation service matches the enquirer's requirements to their eligibility for accommodation available in the area in which they wish to reside. It does not place people or recommend establishments. A small search fee is requested for both services, though this is waived for those on low incomes. EAC's introductory booklet *For you and yours* includes application forms for each service. Two leaflets: *Looking for retirement housing?* and *Choosing the right home* are also available free of charge.

Going into a care home

Sheltered housing is unfortunately no answer for Great-Uncle Archie and Great-Aunt Annie, because one can no longer look after the other even with help from a warden. Great-Aunt Annie can stay in the family house quite a while longer. Where next for Archie? A Home? If so, what kind? And where—near his devoted wife? Or near The Niece?

Residential care homes

Residential care homes are provided by local authorities and by the private (commercial) and voluntary (partly charitably funded) sector. The local authority is responsible for inspecting all of its residential care homes. Local authority homes are usually purpose-built and can be quite large, with between 30 and 60 residents, whereas private homes tend to be smaller and take between 10 and 30 residents. The number of local authority homes is decreasing (although some nursing home groups are indirectly associated or owned at arm's length by local authorities) and it is becoming more difficult to find vacancies. This is because the rapid growth of residential and nursing homes in the 1980s has slowed, and their existing residents are living longer.

Residential care homes offer personal care for older people. The degree of care provided is broadly equivalent to that which might be provided by a competent relative. This would include administering medicines, and helping with washing, bathing, dressing, at mealtimes, and with any lavatory needs, although most people in residential homes can do these things for themselves. Although a residential care home can offer additional help when a resident is ill, it cannot provide nursing care.

It is difficult to make a clear distinction between nursing care and personal care, as often any definition will be based on a combination of care needs, but examples of nursing care needs would be severe mental confusion or very poor mobility. Nursing care requres qualfied nurses, whereas much residential care is carried out by unqualified care assistants. •For more information:

British Federation of Care Home Proprietors   Tel: 0116-264 0095
852 Melton Road, Thurmaston, Leicester LE4 8BN

Elderly Accommodation Council   Tel: 0181-995 8320
46A Chiswick High Road, London W4 1SZ

National Care Home Association   Tel: 0171-436 1871
5 Bloomsbury Place, London WC1A 2QA

Nursing homes

Private and voluntary nursing homes offer a more homely atmosphere than a continuous care ward in an NHS hospital, and although the NHS continues to provide convalescent hospitals, nursing homes are often the only choice for anyone who is defined by the hospital as fit for discharge *(see Chapter 11)* but who cannot cope at home. Most nursing home provision is in the private sector but some have been local-authority financed and many take publicly-funded residents. The independent nursing homes vary in size but usually take between 20 and 30 residents.

The person in charge of the nursing home must be a qualified nurse or a registered medical practitioner, and qualified nursing staff must be available 24 hours a day. All nursing homes, like the 1,600 nursing homes that are members of The Association of Registered Nursing Homes, are registered with District Health Authorities. The DHAs inspect the nursing homes at least twice a year to ensure that health and safety standards are met.

A private nursing home can cost a resident (or the state) anything from £300 to £600 a week, depending on where you are in the country. You can phone the Association of Registered Nursing Homes for a free list of member nursing homes in your area:

Assocation of Registered Nursing Homes   **Tel: 0121-454 2511**
Calthorp House, Hagley Road
Birmingham B16 8QY

Independent Healthcare Association   **Tel: 0171-430 0537**
22 Little Russell Street
London WC1A 2HT

Dual registration homes

These care homes are usually split into two sections or wings. One will have rooms and staff suited to residential care, and the other part will be equipped and staffed to nursing care standards.

RESIDENTIAL & NURSING HOMES

What to look for in a home

Ît is a good idea when looking for a home to shop around. As you will only have a relatively short time to assess the facilities of each home, it is also a good idea to draw up a checklist beforehand. Many homes have a contract that sets out the legal relationship between you and the home. It is very important to read this carefully, and if you have any doubts, have the contract looked over at a Citizen's Advice Bureau or by a solicitor. When going through the contract, you could ask:

- Do you meet the home's 'terms of admission'?
- What are the circumstances in which you may be asked to leave?
- If you were to leave, who would be responsible for finding you somewhere else to live?
- How much notice would have to be given if either you or the home wanted to cancel the contract?

Legal considerations aside, there are other questions to ask, like:

- Are you sure you can afford the fees on a long-term basis?
- What do the fees include?
- Is there an extra charge for the for things like laundry, hair dressing, chiropody and newspapers?
- Will you be near your family and friends, public transport and the shops?
- Is the home accessible and can you easily get around the home and in and out of your room, the bathroom and lavatories?
- Are the rooms single or shared, and if the rooms are shared, would you have enough privacy?
- Can you bring all or some of your furniture and your personal possessions with you?
- Can you lock your room?
- Is there a telephone?
- Can you have visitors, and if so, can they stay overnight?
- What time are the meals served, are these times flexible, is the menu varied, and can your diet be catered for?
- How many staff are on staff on duty, both day and night?

RESIDENTIAL & NURSING HOMES

Choosing a home

A decision is made to stay in Barsetshire, within 20 miles of the family home. (Later, if one of our heroic couple dies and the other is broke, it may be possible for the local authority to 'buy-in' a nursing home place in another county, nearer to The Niece.)

Clearly the best way to choose a home is to visit as many as possible within a 20-mile radius and talk not only to their managers and staff, but to some of the inmates. In most cases the communal facilities and level of care will be the same for everyone. So once a home has been earmarked, the next stage is to have a thorough look at the different rooms inside it, because these can vary enormously and the better ones may be on a waiting list for people inside the home who want to upgrade. Prices may vary by up to £100 a room, depending on whether it is a shared one, a single one, a small upstairs room with no view, or a large one on the ground floor that opens on to a garden.

Having chosen a room in a home that Granny has seen and approved (if she is in any state to do so), and established in thorough interviews with the manager that it is suitable, you can move on to the initial assessment, formal booking and admission. After that, regular visits are needed. No-one should be afraid to complain if an aged relative is being mistreated.

NURSING HOME PROPRIETORS	
The Tusk	*Marbella suntan, hairy chest, gold rings. Drives large metallic-bronze car. Could be making quite a lot out of Granny.*
The Matron	*Caring from ear to ear. Takes your arm when you visit, as if you too have advanced dementia. Always makes you feel guilty.*
The Suit	*Slick, pin-striped, and efficient. Glamorous PA wears Nicole Farhi. About to float his nursing home company on the stock market.*
The Eccentric	*Wears a bow tie and tap-dances at your first interview. Drops names of famous former inmates. Oldies have to listen to Barry Manilow*

RESIDENTIAL & NURSING HOMES

ASSESSMENT
A typical assessment by a residential care home will cover the
following information to be supplied by the future inmate or his
family:

- *Religion*
- *Mobility*
- *Sight*
- *Medical problems*
- *Special needs*

- *GP*
- *Continence*
- *Hearing*
- *Interests*
- *Next of kin*

- *Solicitors*
- *Bowels*
- *Appetite*
- *Previous employment*
- *Diet*

An assessment by a nursing home will ask for more details of
medical history and chronic conditions.

A short-term place

Nursing homes tend to have most of their beds full (private nursing home occupancy rates stood at 91.3 per cent in November 1994). So if, for example, a very unwell grandmother is being discharged from hospital at short notice after falling and breaking her wrist, you may find yourself unable to book an ideal place in time. Homes will offer to put Granny on a waiting list until 'something comes up' (i.e. another inmate moves or expires). However, if you find a reasonably suitable short-term place, you

ADMISSION
Admission to a residential or nursing home after all else has failed is
more than just a question of supplying a few name tapes for clothes
to be laundered. It can be deeply distressing, especially if the person
being admitted believes he will never return to his own home.
Resistance can be quite aggressive, and depression can set in. Daily
calls from members of the family may be a good idea, with regular
visits. However, just like sending a young child away to school, this
can make the situation worse—bringing further homesickness, anger
or tears. If there are genuinely kind staff at the home you will be able
to talk to them regularly to find out how things are going. Likewise
they will call you if there is any serious change in circumstances.

will be in a stronger position to negotiate the best long-term place: there will be more time to shop around and you can put Granny's name on more than one waiting list.

Furnishing a room

If a move into a nursing home looks permanent, the home will encourage Granny's furniture, pictures and other possessions to be brought in so that it can be made more like her own home. A private TV is usually important, particularly for someone who prefers privacy to communal viewing.

Extra charges

The weekly fees for a residential care home should cover everything except personal items such as clothes, newspapers and phone calls.

Medical supervision

There should be liaison between the reidential or nursing home and your relative's GP and the nearest hospital in case of emergency. Dentists and doctors can be called out if necessary.

Regulation, inspection and complaints

Private care homes are now regulated and inspected more stringently than 10 years ago. Some proprietors object that they are inspected unnecessarily often by inexperienced local authority staff; others accept that it can be useful to them to demonstrate official approval. It is also a reassurance to older people and their families that private homes are now subject to one announced and one unannounced inspection every year by the local authority.

If you think Granny is being neglected or mistreated (one serious case of alleged maltreatment in 1995 involved the death of a 91-year old woman after she was lowered into a bath of scalding water by mistake), the matter must be raised directly with the home's manager, then, if necessary, with the authority responsible for inspection. In a case where either is unscrupulous, however, the complaint may rebound on your captive relative. So it is advisable to have a back-up plan to move her elsewhere.

RESIDENTIAL & NURSING HOMES

Running out of money

After eight years in a nursing home, Great-Uncle Archie has just £10,000 of savings left. His wife still survives in the family home and wants to remain there. At this point it is worth getting in touch with the local social services department, because the local authority will soon have to pick up the bill. Three points are worth remembering.

First, Archie should buy things he really wants with his last £2,000 (those old volumes of Wisden and a two-year order for illicit deliveries of port), because it is likely to be his last chance.

Second, if he wants to stay in the same nursing home but the fees are above the level that his local authority is willing to pay, you as a relative may be able to contribute enough by topping-up to keep him where he is already happy and settled.

Third, a move. If Great-Aunt Annie is no longer able to visit Archie, he can be moved to a nursing home nearer to his busy niece and her family: the local authority has a certain amount of money to spend on his nursing home place and can use it to 'buy' a place in another borough or county. Clearly rates vary from area to area and the local authority will be able to buy a much better place in Cheshire, for example, than in Surrey.

Fourth, precautions. Good nursing homes or hospices will not let unwily salesmen through the door. But if you have any doubts, make sure you tell the nursing home, before admission, that no-one on or off the staff must pry into your relative's personal affairs or try to sell him or her insurance policies, funeral pre-payment plans or other financial products.

•**Useful information**
Age Concern factsheets
Finding residential and nursing home accommodation
Local authority charging procedures for residential and nursing home care;
Preserved rights to income support for residential and nursing homes
Rented accommodation for older people.

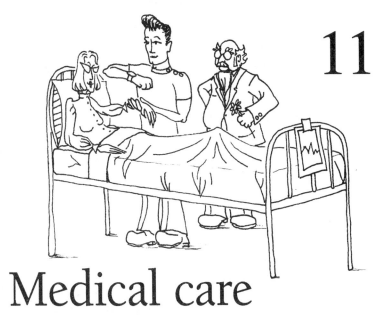

11

Medical care

Now that a 'cradle-to-grave' national health service looks less certain, today's middle-aged need to think ahead more carefully about illness and medical care in old age. This chapter outlines changes in the National Health Service which may affect you, pinpoints the key people in health and medical care for older people, and looks at what is being done about the major diseases of old age.

Fraying at the edges

Old age is often seen as some kind of debilitating disease, and young people assume that anyone with grey hair and wrinkles must be ill or frail. This is not true: most people in their 60s and early 70s, for example, are healthy and active, and many of the problems which older people face are not caused necessarily by their age.

As people grow older, however, they are more likely to develop illnesses or conditions which make it more difficult for them to cope without some help or support, and this is particularly true for people over the age of 80.

One in ten people over the age of 75 is likely to suffer from *Alzheimer's disease* or another form of *dementia*, and one in four

163

MEDICAL CARE

people by the age of 80 will have suffered a fracture due to *osteoporosis*, the process that leads to brittle bones. Specific conditions like these, and others such as *heart disease, arthritis, stroke* and *diabetes*, may lead some people to need extra help. We list these conditions and relevant advisory associations in Chapter 12. But for most people, medical care starts with the local doctor: your general practitioner, or GP.

The GP

A *general practitioner* is the central figure in most people's network of medical support: 90 per cent of public contact with the NHS is with doctors and health centres.

GPs are becoming not only more influential, as they manage their own budgets and shop around for services, but also busier. If you are over 50 and likely to be needing more medical care in the future, it is a good start to get on well with your GP. It is even more important, if your elderly relative is suffering from a chronic condition like a heart problem, to get to know the relative's GP.

If Great-Uncle Archie's gout is playing up, the GP will be able to help not only with medical treatment, but by recommending visits from a district nurse or occupational therapist. He or she can also be the starting point for referring him to the local social services department for an assessment of special needs (*see Chapter 8*).

When Archie collapses into his soup at the regimental dinner and is taken into hospital with a minor heart attack, you, the niece, may be glad you got to know his GP. You may find yourself talking to the doctor regularly as your great-uncle moves from a main hospital to a convalescent hospital or nursing home and then back home.

When, after two weeks at home, Great-Uncle Archie falls and breaks an arm, Great-Aunt Annie calls the GP and again he is collected to go into hospital. His need for subsequent medical care will be assessed before he is discharged from hospital, and by the time he reaches home you will probably begin to get familiar with the process of *assessment* and what happens after. Once Archie is back home, and if he is not able to look after himself, you are entitled to a separate assessment of his non-medical needs (like home help and meals on wheels) from the social services care manager who will coordinate back-up services *(see Chapter 8)*.

The health centre

The building where your GP is likely to have his surgery along with those of his partners, is now often known as a health centre. Some recent changes should make it easier for you, a long-distance relative, to keep informed about a case:

• *Computerised records* will make it easier to access information faster if, say, a grandparent has lost her pills and is confused about replacing them. In the future ir may be possible to issue patients with a simple plastic card bearing all their medical history and treatment details, which can be 'swiped' through a terminal.

• *Nurses* Nurses are now allowed to take on some of the GP's former duties, like taking blood pressure. However, if you feel you really do need to see the doctor, you only have to say so.

• *Transport* Transport to a doctor's surgery or outpatient's clinic can be arranged for people who are not fit enough to drive.

• *Visits* In mid-1995 a new deal was to be arranged between the NHS and GPs so that doctors would be paid a higher fee for going out to see a patient after surgery hours. This may make your GP a bit less reluctant to to winch Great-Uncle Archie off

---

FUNDHOLDING DOCTORS

Nearly a third of the country's 33,000 GPs have joined the government's GP fundholding scheme. The level of funding depends on the number of patients registered by the fundholding GP—for example, two fundholding GPs in one London borough had a 1994-1995 budget of £1,818,000 to pay for prescriptions, staff, and hospital and community services. The Department of Health says that almost 40 per cent of NHS patients now have a fundholding GP, and that fundholders control 9 per cent of the total health budget. However more than 60 per cent of GPs are not fundholders, and District Health Authorities (DHAs) are still the main purchasers of secondary and tertiary care in the 'internal market.

MEDICAL CARE

the floor at 2.30 in the morning to see if any bones are broken, but only on an occasional basis. If a GP is being called out after surgery hours every month, for example, you may be politely told that it is time for him to have a night nurse or go into a residential or nursing home. However, everyone has a right to medical care, and you can insist on a home visit if it is really needed.

Fundholding, the GP and the hospital: what difference does it make?

Government ministers have always emphasised that, whatever the age of the patient, there are no exceptions to the fundamental principle that the NHS is there to provide services for everyone on the basis of clinical need.

However, from time to time allegations arise that older people meet discrimination when they are trying to get access to NHS services. It is difficult to identify the scale of this problem. From the evidence available it would appear that coronary care is the specialty where discrimination against older patients is likely to occur. A survey carried out by two consultant physicians in 1991 found that 20 per cent of the coronary care units (CCUs) surveyed operated age limits for admission for drug treatment, for example.

There is also a problem with timing. Under the new internal market system you can stand less of a chance of getting an operation performed if you need to be admitted to hospital at the end of the financial year. What can one say to this? Simply that if you or an ageing relative has a condition that is likely to need hospital treatment, it helps to get in the queue as early as possible.

The NHS structure simplified

The GP fundholders in their health centres buy certain types of primary medical care for their patients (like district nursing, health visiting, and chiropody). GPs are given the money to buy these services and develop their practices by FHSAs (Family Health Service Authorities). By 1 April 1996 the *family health service authorities* were due to have merged with the *district health authorities* (DHAs) to form unified *health authorities*, although many such mergers had already taken place, unofficially, in 1995.

DHAs are responsible for assessing the health needs of a district's population and buying the necessary services from the four types of organisation which 'provide' them: hospitals or community services still under DHA control; NHS trusts; private healthcare suppliers; and voluntary agencies. DHAs and FHSAs are merging in response to government legislation, and one effect may be that they will have greater financial muscle when buying care services. Authorities will be influenced in their decisions on what services to buy by the range and type of services provided by hospitals, and they will monitor and pay GPs.

The GP, whether he or she is a fundholder or not, is ideally placed to influence care purchasing decisions. This has been summed up by Derek Day, Deputy Director of the National Association of Health Authorities and Trusts, in a comment to the Independent Healthcare Association: "We believe it is crucial for all purchasing that it is influenced by GPs because they have the best up-to-date knowledge of the patients' needs. Referrals by GPs are the trigger for all secondary care services and their views should be taken into account".

167

MEDICAL CARE

The patient's charter

Here are some salient extracts from *The Patient's Charter & You*, produced by the Department of Health (F82/005 1687 1P Jan 95)

ACCESS TO SERVICES You have the right to:
- receive health care on the basis of your clinical need, not on your ability to pay, your lifestyle or any other factor;
- be registered with a GP and be able to change your GP easily and quickly if you want to;
- get emergency medical treatment at any time through your GP, the emergency ambulance service and hospital and emergency departments; and
- be referred to a consultant acceptable to you, when your GP thinks it is necessary, and to be referred for a second opinion if you and your GP agree this is desirable.
- See your medical records

RIGHTS FOR OLDER PEOPLE: Health checks: you have the right to:
- ask for a health check if you are between 16 and 74 and have not seen your GP in the last three years; and
- be offered a health check once a year in your GP's surgery, or at your own home if you prefer, if you are 75 or over.

EXPECTATIONS FOR OLDER PEOPLE: Operations:
- For hip or knee replacements and cataract operations, a waiting time guarantee of 18 months has been established.
- From April 1995 the NHS was to broaden this 18-month guarantee to cover all admissions to hospital.
- From April 1995, you should expect treatment within a year for coronary bypass grafts and some associated procedures (and more urgently if required).
- Your operation should not be cancelled on the day you are due to go into hospital or after you go in unless, for example, the hospital is dealing with a major road accident.
- **Outpatient waiting times:** From April 1995, expect a hospital to see you within 13 weeks of being referred by your GP or dentist.

Free leaflets also available from the Association of Community Health Councils (30 Drayton Park, London N5 1PB) include: *Your Health: Your Rights* •*Family Doctors* • *Care in the Community* • *Making Choices: finding out about your illness and consenting to treatment* • *Going into Hospital* • *Making a Complaint.*

MEDICAL CARE

Hospitals

These divide into different categories:

Teaching hospitals

These hospitals usually operate as district general hospitals but are also centres of undergraduate or postgraduate medical research and carry out the important function of teaching medical students to be the next generation of doctors. For example, St Thomas's Hospital, opposite the House of Commons in London.

Specialist hospitals

Some of these exist already, such as eye hospitals and hospitals for tropical diseases. Some new types are proposed, for example, specialist cancer treatment centres which may be attached to existing hospitals.

Community hospitals

Hospitals which can take post-operative and other patients into convalescence. There are still some within the NHS, usually former cottage hospitals or sanatoria.

Hospices

There are 142 voluntary hospices in the UK, as well as 26 managed by the NHS and 20 run by the Marie Curie Cancer Care and Sue Ryder charities. Most hospices care for people who are terminally ill although, as more people prefer to die at home, the hospices are providing more outpatient care. If a voluntary hospice takes in a very ill member of your family, it is usual practice to give a generous contribution to the charity if you can afford it.

Privately-funded hospitals

These are independent of the NHS system although NHS consultants operate in both types of hospital. Patients going into private hospitals like the Nuffield hospitals or any of the BUPA hospital, are usually having their treatment paid for by private healthcare insurance schemes such as those run by BUPA, Private Patients Plan or general insurance companies like Norwich Union. BUPA has 29 hospitals compared to the 34 hospitals owned by its main competitor, Nuffield Hospitals.

Which type of hospital is chosen for non-urgent treatment will

MEDICAL CARE

clearly depend on a GP or consultant's recommendation, on the condition needing treatment and on the availability of finance. Anyone who needs urgent medical treatment will be taken into the nearest NHS hospital which is able to take in the patient for that purpose.

The hospital overflow

The hospital lies at the heart of current fears that elderly people will not be looked after by the state when they can no longer look after themselves. The reason for this is that between 1990 and 1994 the number of continuing care beds in NHS hospitals dropped from 73,000 to under 60,000. Because chronically ill or post-operative elderly people tend to occupy many of these beds it can be assumed that this group has suffered most.

Rising demand for costly medical care, financial constraints on the NHS, and the effects of introducing an internal market are all blamed for the loss of so many continuing care beds. According to some experts, this is a battle between health and social service authorities about who pays, not about the cost to the patient. Whatever the reason, patients are being discharged earlier after operations or hospital treatment and sent on to convalescent hospitals, nursing or residential homes or even back to their own homes. It is no comfort to their families that the number of private long-stay beds rose from under 90,000 to over 144,000 during the same period, because in many cases private beds have to be paid for. These reforms have dismayed the public and provoked a battery of complaints to the *health service commissioner* (or *health service ombudsman*).

Discharge guidelines

In February 1995 the government published guidelines on the care of the elderly and called a halt to geriatric ward closures in NHS hospitals, asking health authorities to reinstate continuing care beds where they had closed too many.

The guidelines, however, went on to say that hospitals should be able to send patients home if they refuse to move to a nursing or residential home because of the expense: "Where patients have been assessed as not requiring continuing in-patient care, as now, they do not have the right to occupy indefinitely an NHS bed... they do, however, have the right to refuse to be discharged from NHS care into a nursing home or residential care home".

Patient's rights: hospital discharge

There is an appeals procedure to follow should you refuse to leave hospital for means-tested residential care. After the appeal and 'after consultation with the health authority, social services department and, where necessary housing authority', you could be sent home with a package of community care services, instead—which if you do not want to stay in hospital or go into residential care will be the solution you are looking for.

You or your elderly relative will almost certainly have to pay a charge for the 'social care' element of the package *(see Chapter 8)* These charges vary considerably from one local authority area to another, as does the reliability of the services. They are, however, much cheaper than paying commercial rates for help services. The quotations above come from the government guideline document *NHS Responsibilities for meeting continuing care health needs*.

•This is free and is available from: The Health Publications Unit Heywood Stores, Manchester Road, Heywood, Lancashire L10 2PZ. Tel: 01706-366 287.

MEDICAL CARE

Patient's rights: health services

The *NHS Patient's charter*, published by the government and available from your GP, sorts out some of the confusion about what services doctors and hospitals *must* provide and what they should be *expected* to provide. Unfortunately 'expectations' are a grey area and there are still many more 'expectations' than 'rights' for patients (see extracts on page 168).

•Energetic oldies: you can lobby your MP or work with organisations like Age Concern and Help the Aged to raise more 'expectations' to 'rights'. Contact the relevant organisations to find out how. *(See Chapter 5)*

Complaints

If you want to make a complaint about the NHS services provided by your optician, dentist, chemist or GP, you can take your case to the *family health services authority* (FHSA), although a complaint to the FHSA must be made within 13 weeks of the incident. FHSAs manage the NHS services. Pursuing a complaint can take many months and it can be good to have moral support. Your local *community health council (see page 170)* can offer advice and support and help you put your complaint to the FHSA.

If you have a complaint about the standard of care in hospital you should speak or write to the hospital's *complaints officer*. If a doctor behaves unethically or unprofessionally you can complain to the GMC, and if you believe that a nurse or health visitor has acted in an unprofessional way, you can complain to the Council for Nursing, Midwifery and Health Visiting:

The General Medical Council (GMC)   **Tel 0171-580 7642**
44 Hallam Street, London W1N 6AF.

The UK Central Council for   **Tel 0171-637 7181**
  Nursing, Midwifery and Health Visiting
23 Portland Place, London W1 3AF.

The Health Service Ombudsman can investigate complaints about maladministration or the failure of the NHS to provide and maintain a service that it has a duty to provide.

Health Service Commissioner (Ombudsman)   Tel 0171-276 3000
Church House, Great Smith Street, London SW1P 3BW.

Nurses and care workers

When older people are chronically ill, they are likely to come into regular contact with nurses in hospital or in a GP's surgery; or likely to need to recruit private nurses for part-time or full-time nursing care at home. The definitions below apply to nurses working in hospitals, with GPs or for nursing agencies. The helpers that social service departments can arrange to visit your home are social workers, occupational therapists or care workers.

Registered general nurse

RGN, previously known as SRN, standing for *state registered nurse*. An RGN is a fully qualified nurse who can attend to all the nursing needs of a client.

Enrolled nurse

EN, previously known as SEN or *state-enrolled nurse.* ENs have a year's less training than RGNs and usually carry out more limited tasks. One difference between the two is that RGNs go on to supervision and management training.

Health care assistant

Previously known as 'auxiliaries' or even 'auxiliary nurses', *health care assistants* are trained in hospitals but are not qualified. They work under the supervision of qualified nurses, and may do most of the general caring tasks of an RGN or EN but are unlikely to administer oxygen or injections.

Care assistant

Care assistants are often trained in a residential home for older people; or they may have been on a local training course. Care assistants can carry out general caring tasks, like helping people with washing, dressing or eating, and may help with domestic tasks like cooking if it is part of the job.

MEDICAL CARE

Nursing agencies

There are private nursing agencies which are always ready to provide cover. Nursing agencies employ RGNs, ENs, health care assistants and, occasionally, care assistants. The agency will either advertise for the carer you need or have its own lists of available care assistants and nurses.

Most agencies charge an hourly rate that varies depending on the qualifications and experience of the nurse or care assistant required. Some agencies refuse to give any indication of their charges over the phone, insisting that they need to assess a case first. Press the agency hard if it does this, by asking at least for some rough figures. If the company has nothing to hide, it should tell you.

Nursing agency charges covers the carer's pay and the agency's commission. Alternatively, if you only need a carer or nurse for a few hours a day, an agency may charge a visit rate. This means that usually you are charged extra for the first hour or twice the hourly rate for the few hours needed.

There will be other additions to the fixed or hourly rate charged by a nursing agency, like VAT, travel expenses, and extra charges, sometimes more than double the usual rate, for working on weekends and public holidays. Many agencies are used only on a short-term basis, for example to care for someone who is recovering from an operation, and so set their fees at a high level to compensate for this. However, they may be prepared to reduce their fee if told that they are to be used on a long-term basis—for example if someone who is chronically or terminally ill decides to live at home with constant nursing care rather than stay in a home or hospital.

With or without a renegotiated fee, being looked after at home by a private agency nurses will cost much more than staying in a nursing home. To employ two nurses to provide day and night cover on shifts for a single patient is likely to set you back more than £500 a week.

Nursing agencies are registered with a local authority's company registration department. You can get a list of agencies

174

in your area from this department, or you can check in your telephone directory. For further details of nursing qualifications and codes of practice, you can contact either:

The Royal College of Nursing   Tel: 0171- 872 0840
20 Cavendish Square, London W1M 0AB
or:
The United Kingdom Central Council for   Tel: 0171-637 7181
   Nursing Midwifery and Health Visitors
(UKCC) 23 Portland Place, London W1N 3AF

There are about 600,000 nurses on the UKCC's register but some are 'resting', not actually practising. The UKCC estimates that about 500,000 are practising, with about 400,000 of those working in the NHS and some 100,000 (a rising trend) in the independent/private sector, including practice nurses attached to GP's surgeries. The ratio of public sector to private sector nurses is likely to tip in favour of the private sector in future.

Nursing agencies
Nursing agencies also supply nurses who are registered in other countries, for example, Australia and New Zealand. The agencies vary in size and coverage, but here are a few names:

Anzac Nursing Services   Tel: 0171-352 2383
297 King's Road, London SW3 5EP

Associated Nursing Services   Tel: 0171-924 3026
1 Battersea Square, London SW11

Nightingale Nurses   Tel: 0171-833 3952
2 Tavistock Place, London WC1H 9RA

ANZAC is a small agency (around 100-150 nurses) operating mainly in London but supplying live-in nurses in other parts of the UK. Its nurses are mainly from Australia and New Zealand who tend to come to the UK in the summer months looking for

MEDICAL CARE

work. Fans of Antipodean nurses say they are more willing than British nurses to help with a few jobs around the house as well as providing nursing care. Nightingale Nurses employs between 500 and 700 registered nurses and auxiliaries to provide nursing care in hospitals and in the community. The agency will not employ auxiliaries unless they have at least six months experience of acute hospital care.

Employment agencies

Domestic helpers and care assistants can also be found by contacting employment agencies. These agencies will also charge by the hour, but their rates will not be as high as they would be for nurses. Using a private nursing agency or an employment agency can be expensive, so it's a good idea to shop around for services, and it is always worth asking for an all-inclusive quotation, that includes all the agency's charges.

Using only commercial agencies can leave a person vulnerable. For although such agencies are listed and the qualifications and experience of their nurses and carers are registered, there is not yet any official inspection or registration of domiciliary care agencies. It has been suggested that some people are sent to deal with, for example, incontinent elderly people, who have no more than an brief NVQ qualification or a few days training. So it is important to check that the nursing agency you are using takes up the references of the care staff who will be sent out. Again, details of employment agencies in your area can be found in the telephone directory (Yellow Pages) or the local library.

Public versus private

The number of nursing agencies has increased to meet the demands of a growing 50+ population which in the UK, according to Age Concern, will approach 25 million by the year 2025. Those aged 80 and over are the main consumers of long-term care and will make up 4.5 per cent of the UK population by 2011, compared with 2.8 per cent in 1981 and about 1 per cent at the start of the NHS.

MEDICAL CARE

An awareness of the mounting financial demands that increased life expectancy will make of the NHS is generating many questions about the future of government funded long-term care. However, answers to this dilemma are few and far between. At the moment the government is saying that it is up to health authorities and local authorities to clarify the boundaries between means-tested social care and free health care.

Government guidelines state that health authorities, GP fundholders and local authorities need to work together to ensure that "clear agreements are in place covering their respective responsibilities for arranging and funding care", and "effective co-operation between services to ensure a coordinated response to the needs of individual patients". However both The Relatives Association and The British Association of Social Workers agree that there is a pitiful lack of coordination between the various organisations responsible for providing care.

Fundholders, health and local authorities had until the end of September 1995 to draft local policies and eligibility criteria for continuing care. After public consultation the policies were to be finalised by April 1996, and it was expected that by then people would have a better idea of what is going on. Assessments for care and the services that follow still differ enormously from area to area and people with similar conditions and circumstances have been getting free care in some places but not in others.

Accepting lower standards?

People appear to have grown used to the idea of an under-funded NHS and are aware that waiting lists for many conditions can be very long. But although almost everyone expects the NHS to be able to deliver health care in an emergency, fewer people seem to expect the same of the NHS's ability to provide health care for non-urgent conditions.

In April 1994 Mike Norris, London regional officer of the Industrial Orthopaedic Society, summed it up in the *Health Service Journal* : "In the past year or two as the NHS has had more problems we have detected a change in attitude. People are slowly realising the NHS is not going to meet all their needs, particularly in places like London, where there are long waiting lists."

177

MEDICAL CARE

Growth of the independent sector

This gap between what the NHS should be able to do and what it can actually afford to do for older people is being filled by an expanding independent sector. The private sector's current annual turnover is £11.7 billion, or 24 per cent of all spending on health care. and according to the Independent Healthcare Association's (IHA) contribution to consultations on the Labour Party's *Health 2000* report, independents provide 20 per cent of all elective surgery, including 20 per cent of all coronary heart bypass operations and 30 per cent of all hip replacements.

The IHA also claims that the independent sector views elderly care as an expanding and guaranteed market and now provides 72 per cent of all care. At present the private health care industry employs nearly 500,000 people and provides over 400,000 beds for treatment and long-term nursing and residential care, and is moving into other forms of care such as domiciliary and day care and respite services. (Statistics taken from the Independent Healthcare Association's contribution to consulations on the Labour Party's Health 2000 report).

Finally, here are the names and addresses of some organisations which you may find useful if you have difficulties dealing with any issues concerning the health, medical or social welfare of older people, or if you want to get a second opinion about procedures or organisations.

More organisations

British Association of Social Workers (BASW)   Tel: 0121-622 3911
16 Kent Street, Birmingham B5 6RD

British Medical Association (BMA)   Tel: 0171-387 4499
B.M.A. House, Tavistock Square,
London WC1H 9JP

The British Geriatrics Society   Tel: 0171-935 4004
1 St. Andrews Place, London NW1 4LB

12

Ailments and worse

Here we run through some of the common ailments associated with old age, followed by summaries of a few more serious illnesses. The associations listed are well-informed about current research developments, some of which may offer radical new cures by the turn of the century. Giving up bad habits is still a good idea.

Ears and hearing

There are about 7.5 million people in the UK with some degree of hearing loss, about 17 per cent of the population. The most common cause of deafness is simply the ageing process, and at least three quarters of these people are over 60 years old. If you think that you have hearing loss then you should go to your GP, and if the doctor cannot sort out the problem, he or she will probably send you to an Ear Nose and Throat (ENT) specialist so that your ears can be properly examined and your hearing tested. There are several types of deafness:

• *Conductive deafness* Conductive deafness is caused by a problem in the ear canal, the ear drum or the small bones in the inner

179

AILMENTS AND WORSE

ear. An ENT specialist might be able to cure the problem by operating on this part of the ear or by giving some sort of medication.

• *Sensori-neural deafness* Sensori-neural deafness means that something has gone wrong with the inner ear or the system that links the ear to the brain, and it is very rare that anything can be done here.

• In many cases of *presbyacusis*, or age-related deafness, loss of hearing, particularly in the higher frequencies, is common and cannot be reversed by medical or surgical treatment. More often than not a hearing aid may be the most suitable form of treatment.

• *Help* The Royal National Institute for the Deaf (RNID) provides an extensive range of services for deaf people and the professionals who work with them. The RNID provides information, residential care centres, communication support services, training, and 'Typetalk' specialist telephone services (*see Chapter 9*), as well as selling a wide range of helpful devices through its marketing division, Sound Advantage. The charity has regional offices throughout the UK. and is developing a network of 'communication support units' which provide sign language interpreters, computer-aided transcription services, deaf-blind interpreters and technical support. Full details of all RNID services are available from the regional information officers or from the information services division in London.

Royal National Institute for Deaf People   **Tel: 0171- 387 8033**
RNID, 105 Gower Street   Minicom: 0171-383 3154
London WC1E 6

HEARING LOSS BY AGE GROUP	
Percentage of hearing loss audiometrically measured	
31 to 40	2.8
41 to 50	8.2
51 to 60	18.9
61 to 70	36.8
71 to 80	60.2
RNID, May 1994.	

Eyes and sight

A great deal more can be done to keep your eyes working than was possible even 25 years ago. Cataract operations, for example, are becoming simple, commonplace affairs that can restore startling clarity of vision.

The three main causes of age-related blindness are cataract, macular degeneration, and glaucoma. These conditions become increasingly prevalent in the 75 to 85-year-old age group.

• *Cataract* Of this age group, 42 per cent have some degree of cataract, a clouding of the lens which means that light does not pass straight through the lens to create a focused image, but is scattered in different directions to create a blurred image. Diabetes, smoking and excessive alcohol intake all increase the risk of cataract. This risk can be reduced by taking small amounts of analgesics (like paracetamol and aspirin) and vitamins E and C. The most effective treatment for cataract is surgical removal of the lens usually followed by a plastic lens implant.

• *Macular degeneration* Of 75 to 85 year olds 39 per cent suffer from damage or misplacement of the macula. The macula is a spot at the back of the eye in the retina that is responsible for the central part of our vision. Damage to the macula results in loss of central vision, leaving only peripheral vision. This means that although you will be able to find your way around, you will not be able to pursue activities that require detailed vision, like reading,writing, or watching TV. As the causes of this condition are not yet known, treatment is not often possible, although some patients may be helped by laser treatment if the condition is diagnosed early enough.

• *Glaucoma* Of the same age group, 7 per cent developed damage to the optic nerve at the back of the eye by raised pressure within the eye. Over the years this leads to progressively poorer vision which, as it often occurs in both eyes simultaneously and with no other symptoms, means that often glaucoma is not diagnosed until it is well advanced. Since there is no cure and damage to the optic nerve is irreversible, early diagnosis is essential

AILMENTS AND WORSE

so that regular checks, eye drops and, if necessary, surgery or laser treatment can keep damage to a minimum and preserve good vision indefinitely. Most opticians still provide some form of NHS service, and if there are any charges for an eye test, new lenses or new frames, they will be nominal. The cost of going to a private optician, on the other hand, is considerably higher.

The RNIB gives advice and information for partially sighted people:

Royal National Institute for the Blind   **Tel: 0171-388 1266**
224 Great Portland Street, London W1N 6AA

Teeth

Although there is a steady decline in denture wearing in the U.K., as oral health improves, 57 per cent of 70 year olds and 80 per cent of 80-year-olds still have full dentures (false teeth) and many other older people have partial dentures. However, dentures or no dentures, regular check-ups at your dentist are essential for healthy teeth and gums, as early examination and diagnosis will lead to more effective and rapid treatment. For those people who have natural teeth, the two main dental diseases are:

• *Caries or tooth decay* This happens when the bacteria in plaque combine with sugar to form acids which eat into the tooth. The risks of tooth decay can be reduced by avoiding sugary foods and drinks and cleaning your teeth regularly with a flouride toothpaste.

• *Peridontal or gum disease* Inflammation of the gums caused by a build up of bacteria and the formation of plaque. Advanced gum disease causes bad breath, bad taste, and loosens teeth which, if the disease is not brought under control, may have to be extracted. The risks of gum disease are reduced by regular and thorough daily brushing.

In April 1994, according to the British Dental Association (BDA), most General Dental Practitioners (GDPs: about 19, 000), were still seeing most of their patients under NHS arrangements. However it cannot be assumed that treatment will be offered under the NHS and patients should always check before going ahead with treatment whether it is under NHS arrangements or not. Family dentists own their practices and have to run them as businesses. They cover their costs by payments for work done and the NHS does not have any continuing commitment to support GDPs, hence the growing number of dentists working privately. However, for people who do not find it easy to visit a family dentist because of disability or for other reasons, there is a safety net provided by the *community dental service* (CDS), which can visit both residential and individual homes.

• For more information about your local CDS you can contact the CDS manager within the local NHS, using the NHS Helpline on 0800 66 55 44.

British Dental Association   **Tel: 0171-935 0875**
64 Wimpole Street, London W1M 8AL

Feet

There are some basic do's and dont's that, if observed, will help keep feet healthy:

• *Daily care* Wash feet daily in warm, soapy water, not in very hot water, and don't soak them for long periods. After washing it is important to dry feet well, especially between the toes. Regular use of a pumice stone after bathing should help remove any callouses (hard skin). Corn plasters and lotions contain strong acids that may well damage the foot, as can trying to cut away hard skin with a razor or a pair of scissors. Toe nails should be cut straight across, but not cut too short, and preferably after bathing, when the nail is soft. Dry skin can be treated with E45 cream, and moist skin can be dealt with by a few dabs of surgical spirit, especially between the toes.

• *Special problems* People with diabetes are more vulnerable to foot problems than others. This is because the nerves in a foot of someone with diabetes may become defective. This can lead to a loss of feeling in the foot and/or a deformed foot, due to the paralysis of the small muscles in the foot. Also circulation may be poor, and the feet might be painful, especially at night. Poor circulation of blood to the feet may mean that there is insufficient blood to clear up any infection, so that minor wounds only heal slowly, if at all. Minor injuries can be treated with a mild antiseptic and a clean dressing. More serious injuries should be treated by a chiropodist. To keep feet in good condition, it is important to keep feet clean and dry, and avoid injuries to feet by never walking around barefoot or in sandals, or digging down the side of toe nails or cutting them too short. With poor feeling in the feet it is vital not to damage feet inadvertently. So it is better not use a hot water bottle or sit too close to the fire, and always to check with a thermometer that bathwater is not too hot.

• *Footwear* Recommended footwear includes natural fibre cotton socks and shoes with leather uppers that will allow the feet to 'breathe'. Ill-fitting shoes are a major cause of poor foot health, and it is vital to ensure that shoes fit properly by having feet measured both in length and width. Price is not always a guarantee of good footwear, and the fit of the shoe is more important than the shoe size you think you have.

• *Treatment* If *anything* is painful, consult a state-registered chiropodist (SRC). An chiropodist will have undergone a minimum three or four year full-time training course, resulting in a qualification that is recognised by the Department of Health. All chiropodists working in the NHS hold this qualification. Chiropodists are able to offer advice and treatment where appropriate, on a full range of conditions (corns, callouses, fungal infections like athlete's foot, verrucae, nail problems) and can provide more specialist treatments (such as examination of foot malfunction, provision of appliances like insoles, nail surgery, and any other foot or lower limb problems).

• *Help* For books and leaflets on caring for feet, as well as details of local chiropodists, contact:

The Society of Chiropodists   **Tel: 0171-486 3381**
53 Welbeck Street, London W1M 7HE.

And worse...

Small problems at your extremities are one thing, but some other things that can happen in old age are not so easily laughed off.

Urinary incontinence

Between 3 and 3.5 million people in the UK suffer from urinary incontinence. More than half of those affected are over 65, and most of them are women. Urinary incontinence affects between 10 and 20 per cent of older people in the community, 35 per cent of those in long-term hospital care, and 50 per cent of those in nursing homes. At present the NHS spends approximately £80 million a year coping with incontinence, and as the elderly population grows, so will treatment costs. It is thought that current expenditure treats only a minority of sufferers as the majority will not seek help owing to the embarrassing nature of the problem. There are many types of incontinence, some more difficult to treat than others. The three main types are:

• *Urgency* No prizes for guessing that this is when the bladder needs to be emptied in a hurry and the person is often unable to get to the lavatory in time, especially if the he or she has difficulty getting around.

•*Frequency* When the bladder can only hold a small volume and has to be emptied very often. Frequent emptying of the bladder can become a habit which, in time, may prevent the bladder from stretching to its full capacity and so make the problem worse.

•*Leakage* When a small amount of urine leaks from the bladder, before or after a visit to the lavatory. This is often due to weakness of the pelvic floor muscles or a change in the position of the bladder and urethra, which can occur in pregnancy, childbirth, or after surgery.

• *Help* To help deal with incontinence you can cut down on diuretics (these are drinks, like tea, coffee and alcohol, that increase the amount of urine that is produced); try to retrain your bladder to hold greater amounts of urine by 'holding on' a bit longer each day until the intervals between visiting the lavatory become more manageable; or you can exercise the muscles around your urethra by tightening and relaxing them slowly at every opportunity. If your incontinence cannot be cured, then it can almost certainly be managed. For more help and advice, you can contact:

The Continence Foundation   **Tel: 0171-404 6875**
2 Doughty Street, London WC1N 2PH

Most common illnesses

For every major disease or condition associated with old age there is at least one charity which funds research or gives information and advice to sufferers and their families. You can help by giving money to these charities or by doing voluntary work for them.

Alzheimer's and dementia

The term *dementia* is used to describe conditions that result in the progressive loss of mental functions. Dementia is usually a disease of old age and *Alzheimer's disease* is the commonest form of dementia, responsible for more than half of all cases. The next most common type of dementia is multi-infarct dementia, which occurs because the blood supply to tiny areas of the brain fails, creating dead patches.

What does not vary is the enormous pressure placed on the family and friends of people with dementia, and research is being carried out by the Alzheimer's Disease Society on the best services available to those caring for Alzheimer's sufferers.

NUMBERS

According to the Alzheimer's Disease Society, there are an estimated 600,000 people with dementia in the UK, and the breakdown by age is as follows:

Age	Prevalence
40 - 65	Less than one in a thousand
65 - 70	Two in a hundred
70 - 80	Five in a hundred
Over 80	Twenty in a hundred

AILMENTS AND WORSE

• *Symptoms* Alzheimer's is a physical disease which has a progressive effect on the ability to remember, think and reason. Its causes are not fully understood, and as yet there is no cure. The symptoms of Alzheimer's disease, such as wandering and loss of short-term memory, vary from person to person.

• *Research* The Alzheimer's Disease Society funds several research fellowships, among them a project to develop genetic testing for the disease. In addition, trials are being conducted with drugs aimed at reducing deficiencies of certain chemicals in the brain.

• *Help* Information and advice on medical, legal, financial and welfare issues, plus factsheets and booklets on a wide range of topics, is available from:

Alzheimer's Disease Society (England & Scotland) Tel: 0171-306 0606
Gordon House, 10 Greencoat Place
London SW1P 1PH

Arthritis and Rheumatism

Rheumatism is a general term used to describe aches and pains in the bones, muscles and joints. There are more than 200 rheumatic diseases that fall into four main groups: inflammatory arthritis, osteoarthiritis, soft tissue rheumatism and back pain. Rheumatic complaints needing medical help, like osteoarthritis and rheumatoid arthritis, are said to affect nearly eleven million people.

Arthritis is a disease which attacks the joints, sometimes leaving them damaged, and is the single biggest cause of disability in the UK today. While research has found the cause of some types of arthritis, nobody has yet found a single cure. All forms of arthritis and rheumatism can be relieved by treatment. Because the severity as well as the type of arthritis varies greatly in different people, and at different stages of the disease, treatment has to be tailored to the individual, and can involve periods of rest and exercise, physiotherapy, drug treatment and surgery.

• *Research* The Bristol Royal Infimary has, so far successfully, introduced low-dose steroids to the regular anti-inflammatory drug treatment for rheumatoid arthritis; and work at the Kennedy Institute in London has developed a man-made antibody that cuts out the chemical messenger TNF that is partly responsible for inflammation. The Bristol Royal Infirmary has developed a new blood test for *osteoarthritis*, enabling the disease to be detected and treated earlier.

• *Help* For more information you can contact the Arthritis and Rheumatism Council (ARC). The Council funds over 350 research projects into rheumatic diseases, and publishes information sheets and over 40 free booklets to help people understand and cope with arthritis. Arthritis Care, with 570 branches throughout the UK, is the biggest voluntary organisation working with people with arthritis. This charity runs a national home visiting service, provides professional help and grants for equipment and other aids to living. Also it publishes booklets and leaflets, and runs a residential home for older people with arthiritis, as well as five specialist holiday centres and 18 self-catering units for other people with arthritis.

The Arthritis and Rheumatism Council   **Tel: 01246 -558 033**
PO Box 177, Chesterfield, Derbyshire S41 7TQ

Arthritis Care   **Tel: 0171-916 1500**
18 Stephenson Way, London NW1 2HD`   **Counselling: 0800-289 170**

Cancer

It is difficult to say anything meaningful about cancer in a few paragraphs. However, it is not true that a diagnosis of cancer is necessarily a death sentence. Some people are cured of cancer and many of those who are not cured still lead full and active lives. There are about 200 different types of cancer, and many of them can be treated successfully if they are detected early enough.

Several tests can be carried out before a course of treatment is suggested, and the type of test depends in part on your symptoms. A test may involve a small surgical procedure called a biopsy, a blood test or an X-Ray or scan. Treatment varies from person to person, depending on the type of cancer, but may involve the use of radiation treatment (radiotherapy), surgery, or drugs (chemotherapy).

• *Treatment* A reorganisation of cancer treatment within the NHS is likely to take place over the next few years. High-technology treatment will be concentrated in specialised cancer centres. This means that cancer beds may be phased out at some hospitals and patients will be referred to the new centres instead.

• *Research* There is a new field of chemotherapy being developed called monoclonal antibody (magic bullet) treatment, using drugs that affect only the cancer cells that they recognise, so reducing the side effects of treatment on the whole body.

• *Help* Trying to come to terms with cancer and its treatment can be profoundly difficult for those who have cancer, and their relatives and friends. There are over 450 cancer support and self-help groups dotted around the UK, and charities like CancerLink and BACUP offer counselling, advice and information, as well as publishing booklets on the medical and emotional aspects of the disease. The Macmillan Fund is famous for the nursing service it provides. CancerLink was due to concentrate on the elderly from September 1995.

BACUP   Information Service Tel: 0800-181 199
British Association of Cancer United Patients
3 Bath Place, Rivington Street   Admin. Tel: 0171-696 9003
London EC2A 3JR   Counselling Tel: 0171-696 9000

Cancer Care Society   **Tel: 0117-942 7419**
21 Zetland Road, Redland, Bristol BS6 7AH

Cancer Relief Macmillan Fund   **Tel: 0171-351 7811**
Anchor House, 15 - 19 Britten Street, London SW3 3TY

CancerLink   **Tel: 0171-833 2451**
17 Britannia Street,   **Minicom: Use voice announcer**
London WC1X 9JN
and 9 Castle Terrace, Edinburgh EH1 2DP   **Tel: 0131-228 5557**

AILMENTS AND WORSE

Diabetes

The most common form of diabetes that develops in older people is non insulin-dependent, or 'type two', diabetes. This happens because the pancreas produces less insulin than the body needs, and it is insulin that helps the body use sugar to produce energy. Diabetes affects at least 6 out of every 100 people over the age of 65.

• *Symptoms* The symptoms of diabetes can be very general, and include tiredness, blurred vision, changes in weight, feeling thirsty and wanting to go to the lavatory more frequently.

• *Treatment* There is no cure for diabetes but it can be treated successfully by diet, or diet and tablets, or by diet and insulin. Most older people will be treated by diet only or diet and tablets. The diet recommendedfor diabetes is the same healthy diet recommended for everyone: a diet that is high in fibre and low in fat and sugar (*See Chapter 4*). The tablets used to treat diabetes help to lower blood sugar levels. There are three different types of tablets used : *sulphonylureas*, which help the pancreas to produce more insulin; *biguanides*, which help the insulin in the body to use sugar more effectively; and *alpha-glucose inhibitors*, which delay the digestion of sugar in the intestine.

• *Prevention* It is important to have regular medical checks, at least once a year, to detect any problems early on. If you have not had a check-up for some time it is a good idea to arrange one with your doctor. The check-up should include noting blood pressure, weight, taking a urine test (to check blood sugar levels), and making an eye examination and a foot examination. People with diabetes have an increased risk of poor circulation and reduced feeling in their feet. This is why good foot care is very important for older people with diabetes. As well as diet and tablets, exercise may be beneficial also, although you should check with your doctor before starting any new exercise as you may need to adjust your treatment or consider other health problems.

• *Help* The British Diabetic Association has over 400 local branches throughout the UK which offer help, information and support on all aspects of diabetes.

The British Diabetic Association   **Tel: 0171-323 1531**
10 Queen Anne Street   **Careline: 0171-636 6112**
London W1M 0BD

Heart disease

The number of deaths from cardiovascular disease (CVD), including congenital heart disease , high blood pressure, stroke and rheumatic heart disease has greatly declined in the past 30 years, thanks to the great progress made in methods of diagnosis and treatment. However, CVD remains the biggest single cause of death in the UK today, accounting for nearly 300,000 deaths a year.

• *Cause* The single largest cause of death is coronary heart disease (CHD). Nearly 170,000 people died from CHD in 1992, and the main cause of this disease is still not fully understood. However there are contributory factors which limit a person's resistance to CHD. These factors include high blood pressure, poor diet, smoking, excessive alcohol intake and lack of exercise.

• *Treatment* According to the government's white paper *The health of the nation: a strategy for health in England* (HMSO 1992), heart disease and stroke have been targeted as key areas for action. By the year 2000 the government hopes to reduce the death rate for CHD in the 65 to 74 age group by 30 per cent (40 per cent for people under 65). There are similar hopes to reduce the death rate for stroke by at least 40 per cent by the year 2000 (40 per cent for people under 65).

• *Help* The British Heart Foundation supports as many research projects as possible, informs doctors throughout the country of advances in this field, and produces leaflets and videos on all aspects of heart condition treatment, including exercise, diet, surgery and medication. The British Heart Foundation also has an extensive array of factsheets and videos, which are available on request from:

AILMENTS AND WORSE

The British Heart Foundation   **Tel: 0171-935 0185**
14 Fitzhardinge Street, London W1H 4DH

Osteoporosis

Over four million people in the UK suffer from the brittle bone disease *osteoporosis*. During a lifetime your bones are renewed continually by two types of cells, osteoblasts (bone builders) and osteoclasts (bone resorbers). These cells work in tandem to maintain the correct balance between old and new bone.

• *Cause* In a person with osteoporosis the bone-building and the bone-resorbing cells don't work so well together and more bone is lost than can be replaced. This imbalance accumulates with age, so that bone mass begins to decline, the bones become brittle and the chances of a fracture increase as a person grows older. Women are more at risk from osteoporosis than men because on average they have a lower bone mass and a faster rate of loss, between 3 and 5 per cent a year, after the menopause. In an average GP practice of 10,000 patients there are 700 women and 50 men affected or at risk of fractures. Since most fractures follow a fall, however, there are several other age-related factors that need to be considered, like loss of balance and coordination, and declining muscle strength and sight.

• *Treatment* Early treatment for osteoporosis is very important, as once bone has been lost it is very difficult to replace. There are a number of treatments currently in use for the prevention and treatment of osteoporosis, including the use of chemical compounds, but Hormone Replacement Therapy (HRT) is the most established method of preventing bone loss in post-menopausal women. Adequate calcium intake is also vital for healthy bones, and is often prescribed in addition to other forms of therapy.

Exercise, in the form of brisk walking, may be another form of preventive treatment for osteoporosis.

• *Research* Research at Loughborough University has shown that a programme of walking can improve bone quality in the heel bone. Further research will ascertain whether this improvement is reflected at common sites of fracture, like the hip. And in 1995 St. Thomas's Hospital in London was reported to have developed a blood test for genetic susceptibility to osteoporosis, and to be developing a vitamin D treatment.

The National Osteoporosis Society　　　**Tel: 01761-432 472**
PO Box 10, Radstock, Bath BA3 3YB

Parkinson's disease

The incidence of Parkinson's disease is believed to be roughly 1:1000 in the general population, rising to 1:100 over the age of 65 and 1: 50 over the age of 80, and there are more than 120,000 people with Parkinson's disease in the UK today. The disease is a progressive neurological disorder affecting learned voluntary movements like walking, talking, and swallowing.

• *Symptoms* There are three main symptoms : shaking, stiffness and slowness of movement. There is no known cure for Parkinson's disease. However in the last ten years there have been considerable advances in the medical treatment of the disease and it is likely that this progress will continue equally rapidly in the future.

• *Treatment* The main treatment for Parkinson's disease is drug therapy, and with optimum drug treatment, where both the dosage and the timing of medication are tailored to the individual, life expectancy is normal. The Parkinson's Disease Society follows the development of drugs which are more effective and have less side effects, and is sponsoring research into forms of treatment aimed at reducing the progression of the disease.

• *Help* The Society publishes a quarterly newsletter and a whole range of leaflets providing information and advice for those with Parkinson's disease and their relatives and friends. It also runs a Helpline that is open from 10am to 4pm, Monday to Friday.

The Parkinson's Disease Society　　　**Tel: 0171-383 3513**
22 Upper Woburn Place　　　　　　**Help Line: 0171-388 5798**
London WC1H ORA

AILMENTS AND WORSE

Stroke

Each year about 100,000 people in the UK have a stroke for the first time, and 60,000 people die of stroke—it is the third highest killer.

- *Cause* A stroke is sudden damage to the brain caused by a blood clot or haemorrhage, and can cause, among other things, loss of balance and weakness or paralysis on either the left or the right hand side of the body. There are a number of factors that can increase the risk of suffering a stroke, like smoking, heavy drinking and lack of exercise.

- *Prevention* However the most important factor is high blood pressure, and as this usually shows no symptoms it often goes undetected. So a regular blood pressure check is an excellent preventive measure.

- *Research* The Stroke Association is currently funding the trials of drugs that might be able to disperse a blood clot in the early hours after a stroke. It is also funding the study of the effectiveness of an operation which can clear certain narrowed arteries in the neck that may be failing to carry sufficient blood to the brain.

- *Help* The Association has 26 information centres throughout the UK. Their staff can give information and confidential advice on a wide variety of issues and answer questions about benefits, rehabilitation, respite care and welfare grants. The Association's *family support* service provides emotional support for the patient and his or her family, while their *dyphasic support* service works to restore the language skills of those whose speech has been affected by stroke. If there is not yet an information centre in your area you can contact the Stroke Association's advisory service at:

The Stroke Association   **Tel: 0171-490 7999**
CHSA House, Whitecross Street, London EC1Y 8JJ

Funerals, burials and cremation

We hope you won't read this final chapter when anyone close to you is facing death. Death is too devastating an experience to deserve the insult of insignificant advice. But if you are fighting fit, feeling cheerful and simply curious about the mechanics of funerals, burials and cremation, this chapter tells you how it all works.

Letting go

Great-Uncle Archie is dead, and was buried under a tree in a country churchyard after the funeral. Great-Aunt Annie is now 96 and barely able to move from her wheelchair because she is so weak. When Archie died two years ago, part of her soul seemed to go with him. She has talked a lot to her niece, and has told her that she wants to be cremated. Her niece has listened, and will follow her wishes. But she knows little about what to do. Here are the starkest of facts.

FINAL CEREMONIES

Registering a death

If someone dies in hospital, a ward sister will contact the nearest relative or, if there are no relatives, a friend or neighbour. Most hospitals now have a *patient affairs department* that can give advice about necessary procedures and funeral arrangements and will arrange for the nearest relative to collect the dead person's property. Until the relative or friend can arrange for it to be moved, the body is usually kept in the hospital mortuary, but most funeral directors have a chapel of rest in which the person who has died can be held before the funeral.

If the death was expected and happened somewhere other than in a hospital—for example at home—the first person to get in touch with is the doctor who attended the person who has died during his or her final illness. If the doctor can certify the cause of death then he or she will give you a sealed envelope addressed to the *registrar*, which is a *medical certificate* showing the cause of death; and another envelope containing a *formal notice* which states that the doctor has signed the medical certificate and which gives information on how to register the death.

A death must be registered by the registrar of births and deaths for the area in which it occurred within five days, and you can find the address of the local registrar can be found in the phone directory or get it from your doctor, the local council, post office or police station.

However, if the death was unexpected and has been referred to a coroner, it cannot be registered until the registrar has received authority from the coroner to do so. If the death has been referred to a coroner but there is no inquest the registrar will want to see the notification by the coroner: *Form 100* or the *'pink form'*. The registrar will also want to see the medical certificate giving the cause of death and, if possible, the dead person's medical card.

The registrar will also need to be given the dead person's date and place of birth, as well as the date and place of death, and his or her full name, last address, occupation and other personal details—including whether the deceased was getting a pension or allowance from public funds.

196

FINAL CEREMONIES

Burial and cremation forms

In return the registrar will issue: a *certificate for burial or cremation*, unless a coroner has given you an *order for burial (form 101)* or a *certificate for cremation (form E)*. All these forms give permission for the body to be buried or to apply for cremation. The form that you are given by the registrar or coroner should be taken to the funeral director so that the funeral can be held. A *certificate of registration of death (form BD 8 Rev)* is for social security purposes only. If any of the information on the back of the certificate is applicable, than fill it in and send or give it to your social security office.

The registrar can also let you have a *death certificate* if you want one, but you will have to pay a fee. The *death certificate* is a certified copy of the entry in the death register and may be needed to prove the dead person's Will and settle any pension claims, insurance policies, savings bank certificates and premium bonds. It is a good idea to get several copies of this form, as there is a higher charge for copies requested after registration .

Applying for cremation

Once a death has been registered there are additional forms which have to be completed before a cremation can take place, as no-one can be cremated until the cause of death has been definitely established.

If the body is to be cremated and has not been referred to the coroner, the registrar will issue the *certificate for burial or cremation*. Whoever is organising the funeral will then have to complete an *application form for cremation (form A)*, that can be obtained from the funeral director or crematorium.

Two cremation certificates *(forms B and C)*, provided by the funeral director or crematorium, will also have to be completed also. *Form B* is completed and signed by the doctor who last attended the dead person, to certify the fact and cause of death. *Form C* is the confirmatory certificate, signed by a second and independent doctor. There is a fee for filling in the B and C forms. As of April 1994 the British Medical Association recommended a

FINAL CEREMONIES

LOST PROPERTY

Legend has it that in the 1980s boom the items most often found in Japanese railway lost property offices and lock-up cubicles were funeral urns containing the dusty remains of dead salarymen. The reason: the price of land in Japan had soared to such heights that no-one could afford a burial space out in the open.

---

minimum fee of £32 for the completion of each form. However the *certificate for burial or cremation* and the B and C Forms are not needed if the death is referred to a coroner. If the body to be cremated has been referred to the coroner and the cause of death has then been established, the coroner will provide *form E*. This is the *certificate for cremation*.

The last form that needs to be filled is *form F*, the *crematorium certificate*. Whether the cause of death has been verified by a doctor or by the coroner this form is signed by the *medical referee* at the crematorium once he is satisfied that all the procedures have been completed correctly.

A coroner?

A death is reported to a coroner only if:

• The doctor is unable to determine the cause of death; if the deceased has not been treated by a doctor during his or her last illness, or when the doctor attending the patient did not see him or her within 14 days before or after death.

• Similarly, if the person died while he or she was being operated on or while recovering from the effects of an anaesthetic; or died suddenly in an accident or in unexplained circumstances, then they too would be referred to the coroner.

• A coroner will also have to ascertain the cause of death if the person has died as a result of an industrial injury, an act of violence, poisoning, neglect or abortion, or when the death has occurred in prison or police custody.

•**Useful information**

The DSS publishes its invaluable leaflet D49 *What to do after a death*. This concise booklet shows what administration needs to be done after a death and how to go about it, and is available from your local social security office or from: The D.S.S. Leaflets Unit PO Box 21, Stanmore, Middlesex HA7 1AY.

Burials and cremation

Cremation became legal in the UK in 1902, with the passing of the *Cremation Act,* and is recognized by public health authorities as the most hygienic method of disposing of the dead. Most towns have a crematorium or one nearby.

Cremations are becoming increasingly popular, according to the National Association of Funeral Directors (NAFD). Figures released by the Office of Population Censuses and Surveys (OPCS) showed that 453,045 of the 644,784 funerals held in the UK in 1993 were cremations rather than conventional church burials—70 per cent of the total.

Cremations are cheaper than burials, but the cost of cremation is rising. Because of the introduction of the 1990 *Environmental Protection Act,* which requires crematoria to install new incinerators to reduce pollution, the bill for cremation can include an environmental surcharge of anything between £10 and £60. In 1994 the average basic fee for a cremation was just under £140.

The cremation service

The service for cremation is the same as that for a church burial, apart from the form of the committal sentences. Generously, the church will allow a burial service to take place in a church even if the person who has died did not often attend. The burial service can be followed by a short committal service in the cemetery or churchyard. Similarly, a cremation service can be held in a local church, followed by a committal service in the crematorium chapel—or the whole service can be held in the crematorium.

On the day of the funeral the coffin is brought into the crematorium chapel and placed on a trestle, known as a catafalque, and the service begins. The service lasts approximately 20 minutes, after which the committal words are spoken and the coffin is either placed in the grave or, if the service is to be a cremation, hidden from view, usually by a curtain.

FINAL CEREMONIES

After the cremation committal service the coffin is moved into a room where the name plate on the coffin is checked with the cremation order and the coffin is labelled. The body is cremated immediately after the service but, if this is not possible, certainly on the same day. The ashes then are removed from the cremator, allowed to cool and taken to the preparation room, where they are reduced to a fine white ash that weighs anything between five and seven pounds.

A church minister can perform a brief ceremony as the remains are strewn in the crematorium grounds or taken in an urn to be scattered elsewhere, like a private garden. As of January 1995 there is a local charge of £95 to bury cremated remains in a churchyard, and £70 to scatter the ashes in a churchyard. If ashes are to be scattered outside crematoria, churchyards, cemeteries or private property, then it would be wise to seek permission from the relevant authorities and stick to any local regulations.

Financing a funeral

Burial can be fairly expensive, and is becoming more so as space shrinks in both municipal cemeteries and churchyards. Most people who have lost someone they love would find the idea of shopping around for a funeral unbearable. But if you are very hard up to, you may have to.

If a relative dies in a nursing home, the manager may recommend you a firm of funeral directors—but it is possible the home could be taking commission. The best way of choosing a funeral director is to follow the recommendations of family and friends.

When assessing funeral services, you should check whether funeral directors are affiliated to the Funeral Standards Council, the National Association of Funeral Directors, or the Society of Allied and Independent Funeral Directors. Prices and services can vary significantly and these bodies try to make sure that their members come up to scratch.The Funeral Services Council's client pledge and the NAFD's code of practice state that a funeral director should provide whoever is organising the funeral with a written, itemised estimate of all funeral charges and disbursements. However the Consumers' Association revealed that of the 78 funeral directors that the Association visitedin February 1995, 46 failed to provide a price list, and 23 of them failed to do so when asked again.

National Association of Funeral Directors   **Tel: 0121-711 1343**
NAFD, 618 Warwick Road, Solihull
West Midlands B91 1AA

Society of Allied & Independent Funeral DirectorsTel: 0171-267 6777
SAIF, Crowndale House, 1 Ferdinand Place
London NW1 8EE

Funeral Standards Council   **Tel: 01222-382 046**
30 North Road, Cardiff CF1 3DY

According to 1993 NAFD figures, the basic, no-frills burial that NAFD members are obliged to offer costs £535. This included removal and preparation of the dead, a standard coffin and a hearse to transport it. However this excluded embalming, viewing the body, a limousine for the relatives, or any disbursements incurred. Additional costs such as £55 for the church minister, and cemetery fees, added a further £360, taking the total to £895.

Cemeteries and churchyards

As with funeral directors' charges, cemetery fees vary, depending on the local authority or private company that owns the land in the area. Cemeteries can charge an 'opening fee' of between

FINAL CEREMONIES

£130 and £200 to prepare a single grave, £195 to re-open a grave and, should a casket be used rather than a coffin, there would be an additional fee of around £60.

The available space in some areas is shrinking. For example, in the London borough of Tower Hamlets all the cemeteries were full in 1995, and a grave in the nearest cemetery, in the City of London, cost £600.

Alternatively, you can arrange a burial in the churchyard of the local church, even if the person who has died was not a regular churchgoer. But this depends on whether there is any room left in the churchyard and most churchyards, whether consecrated by the Church of England or any other Church, are pretty full and are expected to be completely full by the end of the century.

According to the table of parochial fees published by the Church Commissioners, a burial immediately after a funeral service will cost an additional £100. If all the churchyards and cemeteries in the dead person's parish or borough are full you can still opt for a burial in another parish , but this will require the payment of a non-parishioners' fee, which can be up to double or triple the amount you would have paid in your own parish.

The Church Commissioners　　　　　　　**Tel: 0171-222 7010**
1 Millbank, London SW1P 3JZ

Burial on private land

If there is no room in either cemetery or churchyard, it is possible to arrange burials on your own land. According to Halsbury's *Laws of England*, as long as the burial is not prevented by a restrictive covenant on the land, which you can find in your property deeds, a burial place 'can be established by any person without statutory authority, provided that no nuisance is caused'.

One way of doing this is to set aside a plot of land in perpetuity for the grave, so ensuring that this is not sold with the rest of the property. Although some prospective buyers may not be too keen on a property with a grave in its garden, and its value may fall, there are no laws yet which can be used to force someone to move a grave on private land elsewhere. However it is advisable to contact the National Rivers Association and your local council enviromental health department before going ahead.

If you would rather not have a grave on your own land, there are five local authorities (Carlisle, Harrogate, Brighton, Burton - upon-Trent and Stroud) which offer 'nature reserve' burial grounds, where a tree rather than a headstone is used to mark the grave. The costs are the same as those involved in a conventional burial, with an extra charge of roughly £35 for the tree.

Unusual funerals

There are no rules about how a funeral should be conducted, and it is quite possible to arrange a funeral yourself and organise a non-religious ceremony. The British Humanist Association publishes information and suggested formats for such ceremonies; and The Natural Death Centre produce *The Natural Death Handbook*, which explains how you can organise cheap and do-it-yourself funerals.

British Humanist Association   **Tel: 0171-430 1271**
47 Theobald's Road, London WC1X 8SP

The Natural Death Centre   **Tel: 0181-208 2853**
20 Heber Road, Cricklewood
London NW2 6AA

Financial help with a funeral

If you think you do not have enough money to meet the costs of a funeral, you can apply *(form SF 200)* for financial assistance from the Department of Social Security *social fund*, as long as you make your claim before or within three months of the funeral. However your local social security office will take into account your own financial situation and that of your relatives and the person who has died when assessing your application. Even if your claim is accepted the maximum contribution of £875 that you can get from the social fund may not be enough to cover the full cost of the funeral, especially in expensive areas like London.

FINAL CEREMONIES

> ### LENIN'S EAR
> *Embalming is a tricky business. The team who looked after the Lenin Mausoleum in Moscow kept his body at the right temperature but once his ear fell off. The arrival of big United States funeral companies in the UK, however, has brought modern embalming practices which are claimed to be efficient. Part of the process of embalming involves draining the blood of the dead and filling the body with an orange solution that replaces its deathly pallor with a healthy pink tinge. After that...*

Funeral pre-payment plans

Some funeral directors offer funeral pre-payment plans. Pre-paid plans allow people to cover their future funeral costs (based on today's prices) and so spare their relatives the financial and emotional burden of organising a funeral.

Most plans are sold to those who are over 70 at an average price of just over £1,000, and can be paid for either with a lump sum or in a series of instalments. The funeral companies then invest your money and guarantee that on your death they will meet your funeral expenses. However, should the person who is making the funeral pre-payments die before having completed the contributions, his or her relatives will have to pay the difference. Plan providers in the UK already hold about £150 million of pre-payments, and this figure is expected to reach £500 miliion in the next five years.

Caveat emptor

In May 1995 the Office of Fair Trading (OFT) published the results of its fifteen-month investigation titled *Pre-paid funeral plans*. The OFT has called for legislation to regulate the industry because pre-paid plans, although they have much in common with pension and insurance plans, are not covered by the Financial Services Act.

Despite the introduction of self-regulatory bodies by both the Funeral Standards Council and the NAFD, the Office of Fair Trading does not believe that self-regulation is appropriate. In mid-1995, therefore, there was little to protect the consumer in

FINAL CEREMONIES

the event of a business failure or embezzlement connected with funeral pre-payment contracts. The OFT has said it wants to see statutory regulations covering contracts so that customers know exactly what they are paying for: "the problem is that people who may be believed to be independent and altruistic actually have a financial interest". If you are concerned enough to want a copy of the OFT report, you can telephone or write to:

Office of Fair Trading   **Tel: 0171-242 2858**
Field House, Breams Buildings, London EC4 1HA

The Funeral Standards Council's regulatory body for funeral pre-payment plans is the Funderal Planning Council, at:

Funeral Planning Council   **Tel: 0141-942 5855**
Melville House, 70 Drymen Road
Bearsden, Glasgow G61 2RP

Complaints

The Funeral Planning Council's code of conduct, published in December 1993, suggests that if you are dissatisfied with how your relatives' pre-payment plan is being handled and conciliation fails or is not pursued, you can refer your complaint to the *funeral ombudsman scheme*, as long as the company you are dealing with is a member of the scheme. Similarly if you are unhappy with the service provided by your funeral director and are unable to resolve the matter between yourselves, you can apply to the NAFD conciliation service. Failing this, you can refer your complaint to the Chartered Institute of Arbitrators' arbitration service, or seek redress in the county court.

The Funeral Ombudsman Scheme   **Tel: 0171- 430 1112**
31 Southampton Row, London WC1B 5H

Chartered Institute of Arbitrators   **Tel: 0171-837 4483**
24 Angel Gate, London EC1V 2RS

FINAL CEREMONIES

The Cremation Society of Great Britain   **Tel: 01622-688292**
or Brecon House, Albion Place   **/01622-688293**
Maidstone, Kent ME14 5DZ

After bereavement

Approximately 600,000 people die every year in the UK, leaving at least 1.5 million people suffering from bereavement. The charity CRUSE offers confidential counselling and support to all those bereaved by death. There are now 192 CRUSE branches throughout the UK, with a volunteer workforce of over 6,000 of whom nearly 4,000 are bereavement counsellors.

This charity also publishes over 100 books and leaflets on different aspects of bereavement. For information about the service that CRUSE provides and the telephone numbers of local branches, telephone or write to the address below. The CRUSE *bereavement line* is open between 9.30am and 5.00pm, Monday to Friday. The National Widows Association provides similar information and advice, and also works to protect the interests of (according to 1992 figures from CRUSE) the 3,200,000 widows who, live in the UK.

CRUSE—Bereavement Care   **Tel: 0181-940 4818**
CRUSE Bereavement line :   **Tel: 0181-332 7227**
126 Sheen Road, Richmond,Surrey TW9 1UR

National Association of Widows   **Tel: 0121-643 8348**
54-57 Alison Street, Digbeth, Birmingham B5 5TH

"The trouble with these guidebooks is that they tell you the price of everything and the value of nothing."

Apologies to Oscar Wilde, deceased

Know someone with A-Levels ahead?
A year off before university?
Plan well in advance with

THE GAP YEAR GUIDEBOOK

New edition published every August

UNIVERSITY ENTRANCE... RETAKES
OFFICE SKILLS... LANGUAGES... PAID WORK
OVERSEAS VOLUNTARY WORK
TRAVEL... EXTRAS
BACK HOME

ORDER FORM

Please send me [   ] copies of the latest edition of
THE GAP YEAR GUIDEBOOK
at **£7.95*** per copy   (*Plus 50p per copy postage and packing)

I enclose a cheque for £............ made out to Peridot Press Ltd at
2 Blenheim Crescent, London W11 1NN Tel: 0171-221 7404

➤Please send the book to:

NAME..

SCHOOL..

ADDRESS...

....

....POSTCODE.........................

Schools: please quote your order number. Orders of 5 or more supplied direct at £6 each plus 50p per copy postage and packing. Copies
can also be ordered from all good bookshops.

THE GAP YEAR GUIDEBOOK 1996/7   Published August 1995
ISBN 0 9519755 6 0   Minimum 208pp PAPERBACK

FUNGUS FREAKS
CHOCOLATE CHECKERS
MEDICAL MILLIONAIRES
SPACE EXPLORERS
BRIDGE BUILDERS
DATABASE DISCOVERERS
ENTREPRENEURS, INVENTORS
DOERS, THINKERS
Universities, government,
business, people, facts, figures

A-Levels ahead? Thinking about a science degree?

Find out what *real* scientists do for a living, in one of our BRILLIANT CAREERS guidebooks..

ORDER FORM

Please send me [   ] copies of the latest edition of

THE BRILLIANT SCIENTIST'S GUIDEBOOK

at £7.95* per copy   (*Plus 50p per copy postage and packing)

I enclose a cheque for £............ made out to Peridot Press Ltd at 2 Blenheim Crescent, London W11 1NN Tel: 0171-221 7404

➤Please send the book to:

NAME..

SCHOOL...

ADDRESS...

....

....POSTCODE............................

Schools: please quote your order number. Orders of 5 or more supplied direct at £6 each plus 50p per copy postage and packing. Copies can also be ordered from all good bookshops.

ISBN 0 9519755 2 8 Paperback 176pp Published 1994

208